Personal-Social
Evaluation Techniques

THE LIBRARY OF EDUCATION

A Project of The Center for Applied Research in Education, Inc.

G. R. Gottschalk, Director

Categories of Coverage

I	II	III
Curriculum and Teaching	Administration, Organization, and Finance	Psychology

IV	V	VI
History, Philosophy, and Social Foundations	Professional Skills	Educational Institutions

Personal-Social
Evaluation Techniques

MERL E. BONNEY

Professor of Psychology
North Texas State University

RICHARD S. HAMPLEMAN

Associate Professor of Education
North Texas State University

1962

The Center for Applied Research in Education, Inc.

Washington, D. C.

Foreword

During the 1950's American education was the object of a heated and nationwide discussion. Quite properly, that decade may be referred to as one of Great Debate and Great Reappraisal.

In general, the criticisms that were voiced with respect to our schools had a salutary effect. The public became better acquainted with the work and goals of public education, and educators examined with increased care the values which motivated them as they worked with children and youth.

By the early 1960's a quiet revolution had occurred in the educational practices that were encountered in numerous school districts and in teacher education as well. Greater stress was placed upon substantive content; there was a lively interest in auto-instructional devices (the so-called "teaching machines"); and a quickened enthusiasm was apparent in discussion and study of the durable topic of grouping for instruction so that the schools might better cope with the problems of individual differences. At least a substantial portion of the current, renewed preoccupation with the challenge of wide-ranging human individuality stems from a desire to stimulate more fully the talented and the gifted children in U.S. classrooms. Additional interest resides in the question of how best to meet the social and intellectual needs of pupils not preparing for college—especially those who are not academically inclined—in an era where larger and larger segments of the high school population contemplate continued education at the college or university level.

It is in this setting of rapid educational change—a period alloyed with a substantial amount of uncertainty—that the present monograph *Personal-Social Evaluation Techniques* makes an important professional contribution.

Dr. Bonney and Dr. Hampleman have done an excellent piece of work in setting forth crisply a wide selection of techniques which teachers can use to study better and to guide more effectively the individual students and groups of young people as they move through their years of experience with public education.

This focus on evaluation techniques is especially important because of the emphasis on the learner. Phrased in another way, *Personal-Social Evaluation Techniques* has the virtue of emphasizing the role of the teacher as a professional student of children at a time when great heed is being given to machinery and to structure as educational panaceas. Better tools, such as language laboratories and television, are important to a degree that is beyond dispute. But teaching aids such as these have real and enduring worth only when employed by the capable teacher who has been sensitized to the nature and to the individual status of children.

Dr. Bonney and Dr. Hampleman have done a first-rate job of compiling a body of well-organized information and data that will help teachers improve the design of their daily planning, guide and report pupil progress, and engage in the process of curriculum development on a basis of research and scholarship rather than mere intuition and hunches.

HAROLD G. SHANE
Dean, School of Education
Indiana University

Contents

Personal-Social
Evaluation Techniques

CHAPTER I

Pupil Evaluation

There are three major purposes of pupil evaluation: it is needed continuously by teachers for planning daily learning activities to fit each pupil's specific needs; it is needed periodically for reporting progress to pupils and parents; and it is needed by the school staff to help them make decisions about revisions of the curriculum.

Pupil evaluation is the process of gathering, recording, and interpreting data about pupils which will constitute evidence of the amount and quality of the progress pupils have made toward achieving the objectives set up for them by the school. If the objectives of the school primarily center around a knowledge of facts and ideas, mental and achievement tests will suffice as an evaluation program. If, in addition, other objectives (personal and social feelings, attitudes, and interests) are considered important, the techniques described in this monograph should also become a part of the program of evaluation.

Until recent years the objectives emphasized have been primarily those of subject matter, which could be evaluated by standardized and teacher-made objective tests. The testing movement began at the turn of this century with the work of a few pioneers on both intelligence and achievement tests. Testing during World War I gave further impetus to the movement. During the period from 1920 to 1940 tests were improved and schools were adopting them for their evaluation programs at an increasingly rapid tempo. By 1940 the testing movement had become firmly entrenched.

Teachers throughout the history of education have always given some consideration to objectives other than those of subject matter. They have been interested in their pupils' learning how to adjust personally and socially to their environment. They have always used, to some extent, some of the techniques described in this monograph in an attempt to evaluate the progress being made in reaching these objectives. For example, interviews, anecdotal records, and check lists have been used for many years. Because the results obtained from the use of these techniques did not yield accurate quantitative scores, so little faith was placed in them that no individual or group had ever seriously tried to study and improve them until the 1930's. At this time, during the height of the developing testing movement, more teachers began insisting that there were many objectives which were a part of their curriculum that standardized tests alone were not able to evaluate.

Two forces occurred which highlighted the issue and resulted in more widespread attention to the problem. These two forces were the work and writings of Wrightstone[1] and the experimentation with evaluation techniques that was a part of the Eight Year Study.[2] In recent years the development of newer techniques has evolved slowly as schools have steadily increased their emphasis on a broader range of objectives and as the training programs for teachers have helped them become more sophisticated in the use of these techniques. Teachers are discovering that the techniques may be used profitably if they know how to administer them and if they are aware of their special advantages, limitations, purposes, and uses.

At the same time that schools were increasing their use of tests and were beginning to experiment with other techniques for evaluating a broader range of objectives, a questioning of the use of the terms "testing," "measurement," and "evaluation" took place. Most of the textbooks which had treated the subject of pupil appraisal were termed "Tests and Measurements." It was not until about 1950 that large numbers of authors began substituting the word "evaluation" in the titles of their books. There is now general agreement about the meanings of these terms. Evaluation is a broad term which includes tests and measurements as well as other evaluation techniques which were at one time not given very serious attention by testing people because they did not yield precise measurement. The term "pupil evaluation" is now used to refer to all the techniques which may be used to assess pupil behavior, regardless of the precision of the measurements obtained.

---

[1] J. Wayne Wrightstone, *Appraisal of Newer Practices in Selected Public Schools* (New York: Bureau of Publications, Teachers College, Columbia University, 1935).

[2] E. R. Smith and Ralph W. Tyler, *Appraising and Recording Student Progress* (New York: Harper & Brothers, 1942).

Scope of This Monograph

In this monograph tests of intelligence, achievement, and aptitude are excluded, as is a discussion of the whole background of testing as an area (construction, validation, programs, and so forth). Tests in the area of personal-social adjustment are, however, mentioned and, in some cases, described.

The scope of this monograph, therefore, is limited to a consideration of those evaluation techniques other than testing which are commonly used to assess pupil behavior, plus tests in the area of personal-social adjustment. Since most of these other techniques are more useful for evaluating personal-social characteristics of pupils than for evaluating achievement and aptitude, in describing these techniques emphasis will be given to the more useful area.

Classification of Techniques

Pupil evaluation techniques may be classified into three main types: observational; self-expression; and eclectic (the case study and cumulative records), which employs all the techniques included in the first two types.

Observational techniques include anecdotal records, check lists, rating scales, casual unrecorded observations, situational observations, motion pictures, television, stenographic reports, and tape recordings. (Inventories are not treated separately because they are considered in this volume to be nothing more than long check lists.) These observational techniques have been classified as observational techniques because they are used primarily by the teachers as instruments for gathering and recording data obtained as they observe the behavior of pupils.

Self-expression techniques are autobiographies, compositions, oral expression, permissive discussion, diaries, questionnaires (actually, all tests are special kinds of questionnaires), personal data blanks, interviews, pupil self-evaluation, dramatic play, role-playing, sociometric techniques, and projective techniques. In all these the teacher in some manner gets pupils to express things about themselves which will serve as clues in evaluating their behavior. Since *use* is the criterion employed in making the classifications, check lists and rating scales become self-expression techniques when pupils are asked to use them in evaluating themselves.

Projective techniques are placed in a separate chapter because they need more detailed description and because they are a special kind of self-expression technique. They make use of more highly structured situations; their interpretation is more complex and difficult; and the pupil is not supposed to be aware of the nature of the evidence he is revealing by his responses. This last characteristic explains why dramatic play, role-playing, and sociometric techniques are also classified as projective techniques. Dramatic play and role-playing are included with informal self-expression techniques because they are easier to describe and use. Sociometric techniques require a separate chapter because of the expanded treatment given them.

Extent of Use of Techniques

There is no study of current practices with pupil-evaluation techniques which attempts to measure the extent of usage. Two studies, however—one in 1948 by Michaelis[3] of forty-four California county school systems, and the other in 1949 by Michaelis and Howard[4] of thirty-eight California city school systems—do offer some helpful information. The results of the two studies have been combined in the following table:

EXTENT OF USE OF PUPIL EVALUATION TECHNIQUES

Techniques Used	Per Cent of 38 City School Systems (1949)	Per Cent of 44 County School Systems (1948)
Tests	100.0	100.0
Cumulative Records	92.0	77.0
Interviews	89.5	71.0
Case Studies	84.2	57.0
Case Conferences	81.6	55.0
Group Discussion	68.4	68.0
Anecdotal Records	63.2	32.0
Observation	60.5	73.0
Files of Sample Materials	57.9	48.0
Questionnaires	55.3	30.0

[3] John U. Michaelis, "Evaluation in California County School Systems," *California Journal of Elementary Education*, 27 (August 1948), pp. 12–20.

[4] John U. Michaelis and Charles Howard, "Current Practices in Evaluation in City School Systems in California," *Journal of Educational Research*, 43 (December 1949), pp. 250–60.

EXTENT OF USE OF PUPIL EVALUATION TECHNIQUES *(cont.)*

Techniques Used	Per Cent of 38 City School Systems (1949)	Per Cent of 44 County School Systems (1948)
Rating Scales	44.7	11.0
Check Lists	36.8	21.0
Inventories	31.6	18.0
Log or Diaries	13.2	16.0
Sociograms	10.5	2.0

Other techniques mentioned only once, by either city, county, or both, are the following: follow-up studies, autobiographies, clinics, case work, stenographic reports, films, recordings, psychiatric consultation, parental interviews, graphs of pupils' progress, interaction content records, and photographs.

How representative the findings shown here may be for the rest of the country is not known. It is probably safe to conclude that tests are used in all schools to a greater extent than any of the other techniques listed, most likely because teachers are more familiar with tests. The teachers in the city systems in California used other techniques more than the county teachers, probably because of more training and/or encouragement to use these techniques.

Need for These Techniques

There are many good reasons why teachers should learn how to use a variety of evaluation techniques other than testing. The following are some of the most important:

1. Recent expansion of the objectives of the schools to include *personal-social behavior changes,* which are not readily measurable by tests, requires the use of other techniques.

2. Informal techniques supply the teacher with valuable data which *supplement* test information and helps to make it more meaningful.

3. The use of many techniques gives a *comprehensive* picture of the pupil which facilitates a better understanding of all his needs.

4. Information obtained from the use of these techniques is better than test results for *discovering causes* of behavior.

5. The additional information obtained about pupils enables the teacher and the schools to do a better job of *shaping the curriculum* to the needs of pupils.

6. These techniques provide illustrative data which are helpful in reporting *pupil progress* to parents.

7. *Feelings, emotions,* and *attitudes* may be evaluated with these techniques.

8. Information about these inner feelings and frustrations of pupils makes it possible to *prevent behavior problems.* Much time now devoted to corrective and remedial work may be eliminated.

9. The intensive study of pupils which is fostered by the use of these techniques gives teachers new insights into *special problems of individual pupils.*

10. Information gathered through the use of one technique can be used to *evaluate the validity* of information gathered by other means.

CHAPTER II

Observational Techniques

Observation as a Method

Throughout history men have evaluated one another in terms of the observed behavior and appearance of those whom they would choose as mates or friends or hire as employees. In recent times, men have discovered that judgments based upon casual observation were not always reliable. Thus, marriage counselors began to suggest that a longer period of courtship was advisable (time for more observations); employers found it better to have several men in the office talk to a prospective employee (several independent judgments); and people found that firm friendships were developed over a period of time and under the stress of many different types of situations (variety of observations).

As more and more people began to make a profession of studying other people, they soon became aware of the weaknesses and strengths of observational methods. Ideas were exchanged with one another and research projects were employed to study better means of evaluation. At the beginning of this century the objective testing movement began. Carried on to the present day, it has attempted to measure with objective tests everything of rather precise measurable behavior. It has found considerable success in the objective measurement of mental ability and academic achievement. It has been less successful in finding highly objective means of measuring the areas of social and emotional adjustment and behavior. In these areas observation is still the predominant method of evaluation, but enough is now known about the better ways of conducting a variety of observational techniques that, if properly planned and executed by trained persons, fairly objective evaluations can be made.

There are many forms of observational techniques, most of which may be classified as one of the following techniques described in this chapter: anecdotal records, check lists, rating scales, casual observation, situational observation, movies, television, and tape recordings. Since the most important of these are dealt with in considerable detail, only a few generalizations about observations are considered at this point.

Definition. Observation as a method of studying pupils consists of the direct observation of the behavior of individuals or class groups.

Observation may be categorized in several ways. First, observations may be casual (no *specific* purpose in observing, fleeting impressions, no recording), or they may be controlled (observe a specific type of behavior, record what was observed). Controlled observations may be subdivided into two groups: the type in which a specific thing is being looked for, but no effort is made to manipulate what the pupils are to do; and the type in which the investigators rig or manipulate the situation. Second, observations may be categorized into unrecorded or recorded observations. Third, they may be classified as individual or group observations.

Observation has come to be known in educational literature as the use of those techniques of evaluation which result in less objective information. While this is the present concept, perhaps it should be pointed out that in reality all data collected for evaluative purposes, no matter how measurable and objective one feels they are, are based upon observation. It may be fairly concluded that over a period of time, as observational techniques become refined so that they yield more precise measurements, they will be reclassified as measuring instruments.

Advantages

1. Observational techniques are a source of data about social and emotional behavior for which precise measurement is not available.

2. These techniques are a part of the teaching process itself, if it is being managed well.

3. Observational techniques are adaptable to almost any kind of situation. They may be used with individuals, groups, children of all ages, and with children of any race or cultural background.

Limitations

1. The process of observing, recording, and interpreting data is time consuming.

2. If the results of observation are to be valid, observers need skill and a clear understanding of the situation and the reasons for making the observations.

3. The presence of an observer, especially someone other than the regular teacher, may cause the subject being studied to behave differently than he would have otherwise.

Suggestions to observers

1. Train yourself to record accurately what you see.

2. Try to leave your interpretation and any biases or prejudices you may have out of the record.

3. Each time you observe have something specific to look for—have a purpose. It is seldom worthwhile to observe *in general*.

4. Observe a pupil over a long period of time and in many different types of situations, so that you are sure that your sample is typical behavior for that pupil.

5. Remember that the behavior you observe constitutes only symptoms—that you will have to have enough background in understanding behavior problems and the types of behavior which are characteristic of children at various age levels to be able to look later at these recorded facts and make intelligent interpretations.

Anecdotal Records

An anecdotal record is a written description of the behavior of a pupil. The originator of the term defines it in this way:

> . . . the anecdote is a record of some significant item of conduct, a record of an episode in the life of the student, a word picture of the student in action; the teacher's best effort at taking a word snapshot at the moment of the incident; any narrative of events in which the student takes such part as to reveal something which may be significant about his personality.[1]

Descriptions of the behavior of pupils have been made by a few teachers, here and there, throughout the history of teaching. Randall, however, at the Rochester Anthenaeum and Mechanics Institute (now the Rochester Institute of Technology) was the first to use, describe, and name a system for keeping such records. Jarvie and Ellingson have prepared an excellent account of the work done there in developing an anecdotal record system.[2] It was there also that the term "anecdotal behavior journal" was first used. Such a journal was simply a running account of recorded "anecdotes."

---

[1] John A. Randall, "The Anecdotal Behavior Journal," *Progressive Education*, 13 (January 1936), pp. 21–26.

[2] L. L. Jarvie and Mark Ellingson, *A Handbook on the Anecdotal Behavior Journal* (Chicago: University of Chicago Press, 1940).

Purpose and need. The central purpose of a system of anecdotal records is to collect data about the social and emotional facets of a pupil's growth and adjustment, areas for which the testing movement had failed to produce satisfactory objective evaluation instruments. This need became more pressing as the teaching profession began to realize that emphasis on these areas of development in children was just as important as the prevailing emphasis on their mental and physical well-being.

The implementation of this purpose in the past has been confined rather largely to the study of pupils with severe behavior problems. Many educators, however, have pressed for the establishment of an anecdotal record system for all pupils, believing that such records would help teachers detect and correct problems before they become serious.

Examples and types. Fundamentally, there are only two major types of anecdotal records: the first, a purely factual account of the behavior incident observed; the second, a combination of factual account and several other things, either mixed in with or separated from the factual material. These other things, which may be present in various combinations, are: interpretation of the incident, a record of treatment already applied, and recommendations for future treatment. The following examples are all taken from Traxler,[3] but the classification by types is that of the authors.

Type 1 (Factual)

> In a meeting of her club today, Alice fired questions at the new president at every opportunity. She interrupted many times during the period. On several occasions the other students called for her to sit down.

Type 2 (Mixed)

> In a meeting of her club today, Alice showed her jealousy of the new president by firing questions at her whenever there was an opportunity. She tried to create difficulties by constant interruptions throughout the period. The other students showed their resentment by calling for her to sit down. It is apparent that she is a natural troublemaker, and I think her counselor should have her in for a serious talk.

---

[3] Arthur E. Traxler, *The Nature and Use of Anecdotal Records,* Rev. Ed. (New York: Educational Records Bureau, 1949), pp. 5–6.

Type 2 (Separated)

   Incident. In a meeting of her club today, Alice fired questions at the new president at every opportunity. She interrupted many times during the period. On several occasions the other students called for her to sit down.

   Interpretation. Alice seemed jealous of the new president and desirous of creating difficulties. The other students appeared to resent her actions. The girl seems to enjoy making trouble for others.

   Recommendations. It would be advisable for the counselor to lead the girl tactfully into a discussion of her relations with the other students in an effort to bring about better adjustment.

Most people who use anecdotal records seem to agree that elements other than reported facts should be separated from the facts and labeled as to their nature. Thus, Type 2 (mixed) represents an undesirable type of record. If teachers use this type, they should be encouraged to read the anecdotes later and either underline or put in parentheses those elements which are not factual.

Advantages. The following list of the advantages of anecdotal records and the subsequent list of uses is a summary of the lists of two writers prominent in this field and includes some of the authors' own opinions:[4]

1. Anecdotal records help contribute to a better understanding on the part of teachers of the behavior of individual children. In the process of using them, teachers begin to look for *causes* of behavior rather than at symptoms; they learn to give an increasingly greater amount of attention to the needs of children instead of concentrating all of it on subject matter.

2. All types of behavior—mental, physical, social and emotional—are to be found in anecdotal records.

3. When carefully written, anecdotal records are our best source of descriptions of behavior.

4. By their nature, anecdotal records collected over a period of time give a longitudinal view of the pattern of a pupil's growth.

5. At the same time, records collected in a short period of time about the behavior of a group of pupils give a lateral view. That is, similarities and differences in behavior among children may be noted.

Uses

1. Such records reveal progress or lack of progress on any observable

---

   [4] *Ibid.,* pp. 26–29; and L. L. Jarvie and Mark Ellingson, *A Handbook on the Anecdotal Behavior Journal* (Chicago: University of Chicago Press, 1940), pp. 6–8.

trait or behavior which the school has set up as an objective for the pupil.

2. These records are not intended to replace, but to supplement, other more objective data which may be available.

3. Anecdotal records may suggest clues to specific items in the curriculum which should be further evaluated and revised.

4. The collected data are useful to the teacher in counseling a pupil about needed remedial work. They are also uesful at this time if attempts are made to have him evaluate himself in the light of his observed behavior.

5. The data are useful when teachers have conferences with parents, as it is much easier for parents to understand specific incidents than vague generalities.

6. Previously gathered data help teachers get acquainted more quickly with some of a new pupil's strengths and weaknesses.

7. This information, if collected and recorded carefully, may be of great value for counselors or clinical workers who may be called in to give advice about a pupil's problem.

8. A summary of anecdotal record information may be used as part of the report about a pupil which is sent to his new school.

9. Finally, a summary of this information may be useful for advising prospective employers about a pupil's fitness for a particular type of job.

Mechanical aspects of keeping anecdotal records

Number of children to be observed. There is no general agreement on the number of children who might be observed most profitably by one teacher. When a teacher is first beginning to keep anecdotal records, it is probably desirable to limit the number of children studied to only one or two. At this time many anecdotes should be collected over a period of several weeks. This procedure also is the one which is most likely to occur in those cases where a problem situation exists and where a pupil is being studied to get clues to the causes of certain behavior.

The situation is different, however, if the teacher already knows how to write these records and is confronted with the problem of collecting anecdotes about all the children in all her classes. The problem is relatively more simple if she is an elementary school teacher who has only 25 to 35 in a self-contained classroom. In this case, at the rate of five to seven anecdotes per day, she could collect one per week for each pupil. A secondary school teacher with five classes of 25 to 35 students, however, would be quite pressed to get one per week, or 5 to 7 anecdotes per class period, for each student. A more reasonable load in such cases would probably be no more than two or three per class period.

Number of anecdotes to be collected. In general, it takes quite a large number of anecdotes, collected over a period of time in many different types of situations, to give a generalized or typical picture of a pupil and his problems. There are many instances, however, in which clues to help in solving specific problem situations may be found in a glance at relatively few anecdotes. Thus, there are no categorical limits applicable to the number of anecdotes necessary. The nature of the individual case will determine the amount of data needed.

When should observations be made? Ideally, observations of the behavior of pupils should be made in many different kinds of situations. Not only should records be kept of behavior in different types of classroom situations, but in lunchroom, playground, and out-of-school activities as well. For records of out-of-school activities the teacher may be limited to reports from parents and others. In such cases, the source of the anecdote should be indicated on the record.

What behavior should be recorded? The best answer to this question is, no doubt, that the behavior which is most typical or which is most significant should be recorded. There are differences of opinion, though, about the best way to achieve this result. Some people who work with anecdotal records feel that the observer should be selective, looking for and recording only those incidents which are significant clues in solving a special problem. Others feel that it is necessary to collect a large volume of anecdotes, thus helping to insure a more typical picture of behavior.

How should anecdotes be recorded? Each anecdote should specify the pupil observed and should be recorded as promptly as possible so that important details are not forgotten. It should be dated and, if it is to be turned in later to a counselor or some other person, signed by the observer. The background or type of situation in which the behavior occurs should be clearly stated so that it may be interpreted properly later.

The form to be used for recording may vary by individual choice. An elementary school teacher who keeps her own records and makes her own summary of them once or twice a year may write them on scraps of paper and throw them into the proper cumulative record folder. Or she may prefer to keep a notebook system, with a page or pages for recording a number of anecdotes about each pupil in one place. Secondary school teachers, on the other hand, would find it more advantageous to use a standard card form which could be filed. The reason for this is that such records for high school students usually are sent to a homeroom teacher or counselor to be summarized, and it is easier to handle numbers of them from various teachers if they are of uniform size and form. In addition to having places on the card designated for name of pupil, date, and signature of observer, separate spaces should also be set apart for the background situation, the incident itself, interpretation, and recommendations.

How should records be interpreted? It should be recognized in the beginning that unless the total behavior of a child is recorded elements of interpretation have already been at work in causing the observer to select certain incidents as important enough or typical enough to record. Since this is true, it implies that the observer should collect many incidents, be skilled in interpreting which behavior is important enough to record, or both.

In order to facilitate interpretation, to make it easier to gain meaning from a large number of anecdotes, they should be summarized. A brief review should be made approximately every six weeks. Significant trends may be discovered at this time which will give leads to help solve a pupil's problems. A complete summary should be made at least once or twice a year, at which time a thorough study and interpretation of these records and all other records should be made. The summary may be completely unstructured, although most workers find it helpful to design a form for this purpose.

The most important single factor to consider in order to insure good interpretation is knowledge on the part of the interpreter of the underlying causes of behavior. This suggests a need for a good background in psychology, where applications have been pointed toward pupil behavior.

Several mechanical items are helpful in making interpretation more valid. One of these items is the need for a large enough number of anecdotes to insure *repetition* of typical behavior. Also, it is helpful if ancedotes can be accumulated from several different observers. Repetition of incidents from only one observer will present a one-sided picture if the one observer used poor judgment in selecting incidents to record. Furthermore, incidents selected from behavior in many kinds of situations will give a better total picture of the child. Types of situations should cover as much other-than-classroom activity as possible, in addition to covering a variety of situations *within* the classroom. For example, incidents of subject matter achievement and personal, social, and emotional adjustment all should be sampled. The time factor alone is quite important. Anecdotes must be collected over a considerable period of time before they give a picture of developmental growth or before there is enough repetition to know whether a certain type of behavior is important or typical.

Limitations or weaknesses. The values accruing from the use of anecdotal records are so great that the following list of limitations should not deter the teacher from attempting them. However, the person who wishes to become proficient in their use should certainly become familiar with their shortcomings. The first limitation contains several items which may be partially overcome by training and experience. The other four are inherent in the method itself.

1. The degree of objectivity, and hence the ultimate effectiveness of anecdotal records, is dependent upon several skills of the observer.

   a. The observer may not accurately see the incident.

   b. The observer may not accurately record what was seen. This may be due to lack of skill or to length of time between observation and recording.

   c. The observer may not see everything that happened.

   d. The observer may see what he wants to see in order to confirm his own biased conviction or hypothesis in the matter.

   e. The observer may have difficulty in distinguishing the facts from his interpretation of the facts.

2. Recorded anecdotes, even quite an impressive number of them, are only a small sample of the total behavior of a pupil. For example, the observer may not have seen the events which precede and follow the incident observed. This would suggest the need for great caution in making interpretations.

3. The nature of the method makes it time-consuming.

4. The method is largely limited to social and emotional adjustment problems. Data observed about other aspects of growth may be recorded, but these should be limited as there are more objective means of evaluating mental and physical growth.

5. Anecdotes do not reveal the causes of behavior which has been observed.

Check Lists

Definition. Check lists are lists of items that serve as a reminder of things in need of completion. On check lists used by teachers, the items are usually behavior traits or skills to be mastered. They serve the teacher in two general ways. First, they may be used in recording observations of behavior, in which case they may justifiably be termed observational techniques. Second, teachers may have children use them in evaluating their own behavior or skills. Used in this way, they may then more appropriately be classified as self-reports or self-expression techniques.

Uses and examples. The uses of check lists have been categorized below into six areas. Such a classification may not be entirely adequate because the possible variations in form and usage are almost limitless. Only one example for each area is illustrated in this volume.[5] Using these as a source of ideas, teachers will probably want to draw up their own check lists, basing them upon their own ideas or on locally determined objectives.

Check lists indicating goals or objectives reached.[6] The following check list is used with primary children as a check on words they are able to recognize. It is adaptable in its present form for use in foreign language classes at all levels and for use with definitions of new words arising in any subject area. The definition may be written on the back of each card.

Check List of Sets of Words Child Has Mastered
(Words on small, individual-size flash cards)

Names	Set 1	Set 2	Set 3	Set 4	Set 5	Set 6	Set 7	Set 8	Set 9
a. Eric									
b. Jean									
c. Sue									
d. John									

---

[5] An excellent source for other examples may be found in *Evaluating Pupil Progress,* Bulletin of the State Department of Education, Sacramento, California, XXI, 6 (April 1952), pp. 125–36.

[6] Used by Mrs. Earl Arnold, Sam Houston School, Denton, Texas.

Check lists of pupil interests, hobbies, problems, favorite books, TV shows, and so forth.[7] The problems in this check list were listed by members of the class. Each child then checked the problems which concerned him. It may be used as a rating scale by asking each child to place an evaluation beside each problem (for example, 3 for a big problem, 2 for a less important problem, 1 for a slightly important problem, and 0 for no problem).

Check List of Problems of Sixth Grade Children

a. Getting along with siblings.
b. Wanting people to like me.
c. Meeting strangers.
d. Watching television.
e. Caring for younger children.
f. Budgeting time and going to bed and getting up.
g. Doing household duties and receiving allowances.
h. Feeling self-conscious (including skin problems and clothes).
i. Visiting people and having visitors.
j. Using the telephone.
k. Eating and table manners.
l. Being afraid of things.

Check lists of detailed skills to be mastered.[8]

Primary Readiness Check List

a. Knows own first and last name.
b. Knows own telephone number.
c. Knows street and number.
d. Normal toilet independence.
e. Buttons or zips clothes.
f. Ties shoes.
g. Accepts responsibility for care and storage of supplies.
h. Independent in cafeteria after first day.
i. Takes home or returns simple messages.
j. Can run errands to office or other classrooms.
k. Can print name.
l. Knows age and birthday.
m. Knows most of best-known Mother Goose Rhymes.
n. Can tell or help to tell some of the favorite stories (Three Bears, Three Little Pigs, and so forth).

[7] Used by Mrs. J. George Macklin, Laboratory School, North Texas State University, Denton, Texas.
[8] Used by Mrs. Wilber M. Neely, Laboratory School, North Texas State University, Denton, Texas.

Check lists of behavior of pupils in various situations. The following is a sample of some of the items which might be included in a check list of the behavior of pupils during classroom discussion.

Check List of Behavior During Class Discussions

a. Volunteers information.
b. Never volunteers.
c. Sticks to point being discussed.
d. Digresses.
e. Interrupts others.
f. Listens carefully to points made by others.
g. Adds comments to reinforce points made by others.
h. Disagreements usually justified.
i. Assumes leadership role but does not monopolize discussion.
j. Monopolizes discussion.
k. Manner of disagreement objectionable.
l. Tactful in disagreeing with others.
m. Usually content with class decisions.

Check lists of the sequence of steps used in performing a task. The following check list is a sample of the steps, of the many listed by Tyler,[9] a student might take in operating a microscope in a botany class. The teacher marks 1, 2, 3, and so on in the proper spaces, indicating the sequence of steps to be taken. The sequence taken by a student is then compared with the instructor's list of the correct order of steps.

Check List of Student Reactions in Finding an Object under the Microscope

Student's Actions	Sequence of Actions
a. Takes slide.	————
b. Wipes slide with lens paper.	————
c. Wipes slide with cloth.	————
d. Wipes slide with finger.	————
e. Moves bottle of culture along the table.	————
f. Places drop or two of culture on slide.	————
g. Adds more culture.	————
h. Adds few drops of water.	————
i. Hunts for cover glasses.	————
j. Wipes cover glass with lens paper.	————

[9] Ralph W. Tyler, "A Test of Skill in Using a Microscope," Educational Research Bulletin, Ohio State University, 9 (November 19, 1930), p. 494.

Check lists evaluating products produced by pupils.[10] Although this check list is used with college students, it is just as appropriate for use at any level where students make wood objects.

Check List of Unsatisfactory Items in Work Product Before Going to Finishing Room

a. Knots	k. Dimensions
b. Lack of Filling	l. Operation Missing
c. Core or Glue	m. Veneer Discolored
d. Joint Shrinkage	n. Veneer Split
e. Veneer Sand-through	o. Rounded Edges
f. Glaze or Burnish	p. Exposed Glue
g. Loose Veneer	q. Coarse Sanding
h. Tear-outs	r. Grain and Color of Veneer
i. Rough Machining	s. Damage
j. Warpage	t. Open Joints

As an observational technique, the check list has two unique functions: it serves as a reminder of behaviors which should be studied and as a substitute for taking large numbers of anecdotal records. Although the data collected through anecdotal records are more valuable than that collected by using a check list, the former is so time-consuming that teachers generally find the check list a welcome replacement for part of the observing they do.

In constructing check lists, teachers should be especially careful to have each item of behavior stated in such a way that it is clearly understood. Instead of using the general term "disobedient," it would be better to say "refuses to obey me."

Most check lists can be rather readily converted into rating scales if some measure is added whereby each item observed is rated qualitatively or quantitatively.

Rating Scales

A rating scale is a special kind of check list in which the items or characteristics checked must be rated quantitatively or qualitatively according to the degree of presence or absence of a trait, the degree of perfection of a skill, or the degree of completion of a task.

Types. There are three types of rating scales in common use

---

[10] Used by Mr. C. C. Davis, Department of Industrial Arts, North Texas State University, Denton, Texas.

today: numerical, descriptive, and graphic. Although some few scales may truly be illustrative of one type, most of those being used today represent some combination of the three. The following examples are not to be considered as models but as illustrations of these types. The items used were taken from a check list (self-evaluation) previously described to show how a check list may be converted into each of the three types of rating scales.

TYPE 1
NUMERICAL RATING SCALE

<u>4</u>   a. Getting along with siblings.
<u>2</u>   b. Wanting pupils to like me.
<u>0</u>   c. Meeting strangers.

Code: *0—Never a problem*
               1—Seldom a problem
               2—Occasionally a problem
               3—Fairly serious problem
               4—Serious problem

TYPE 2
DESCRIPTIVE RATING SCALE

	Never a problem	*Seldom a problem*	*Ocasionally a problem*	*Fairly serious problem*	*Serious problem*
a. Getting along with siblings.					x
b. Wanting pupils to like me.			x		
c. Meeting strangers.		x			

TYPE 3
GRAPHIC RATING SCALE

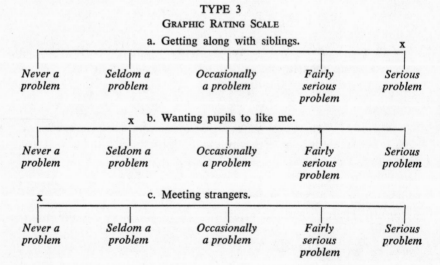

a. Getting along with siblings.   x

| *Never a problem* | *Seldom a problem* | *Occasionally a problem* | *Fairly serious problem* | *Serious problem* |

x b. Wanting pupils to like me.

| *Never a problem* | *Seldom a problem* | *Occasionally a problem* | *Fairly serious problem* | *Serious problem* |

x   c. Meeting strangers.

| *Never a problem* | *Seldom a problem* | *Occasionally a problem* | *Fairly serious problem* | *Serious problem* |

Values, purposes, and advantages

1. Since rating scales give rather subjective results, their main function is to supplement more objective measuring devices. They are of greatest value in those areas where objective measures are the most scarce.

2. With rating scales, it is possible for a teacher to rate a number of traits for a number of students in a relatively short time. It should be considered a supplement to, and not a replacement for, more valuable anecdotal records.

3. As with the check list, the rating scale serves the same function in reminding teachers of traits, skills, and objectives which should be evaluated.

4. Although the rating scale is a subjective instrument, with care in planning and use it will result in more objective evaluation than unorganized teacher impressions.

5. It is relatively easy to construct a good rating scale.

6. Because it is easy to construct, it is readily adaptable to the content of locally identified objectives.

7. It has a variety of uses.

a. Primarily, it is used by teachers in rating pupils.

b. It is also a useful instrument for pupils to use in evaluating themselves.

c. It is useful as a guide to teacher-directed classroom discussion either before or after teacher rating of pupils or pupil self-evaluation takes place.

d. In many instances, teachers let pupils draw up their own list of items to be rated.

e. Some teachers let pupils evaluate one another, anonymously, of course, or let their best friends or parents evaluate them. These evaluations are then compared with the teacher's rating and the pupil's own self-evaluation. Such comparisons make excellent discussion topics for teacher-pupil counseling purposes.

Suggestions for constructing and using rating scales. In this section an attempt is made to make positive statements about constructing and using rating scales. Common faults and errors have been taken into consideration in formulating the following suggestions.

1. For sources of rating scales, look at samples in this book and others on the list of references. Obtain lists of behaviors, traits, and objectives from textbooks and yearbooks of professional organizations. Adapt the items in these scales to your own local needs. Utilize items in your own curriculum guides, or if you do not have them, work co-

operatively with other teachers to prepare them. Scales prepared in this way are usually better than those prepared by individuals. In some cases it is appropriate to let pupils prepare their own informal ones.

2. Clearly define or describe all items to be rated. If possible, each item should be stated in terms of specific behavior which is observable. If more general traits, such as loyalty or honesty, are to be rated, it may be desirable to have a full paragraph description of each item for the use of all who expect to be raters.

3. Check items to be sure that they do not duplicate or partially duplicate one another.

4. Insert a column which will permit the rater to check "no chance to observe" or "not competent to judge."

5. Have at least three persons use the newly prepared rating scale in rating the same group of pupils. Use their criticisms of the items and their differences in ratings to improve the items or the scaling arrangement.

After the rating scale has been prepared, the following suggestions for using it may prove helpful.

1. Be as meticulous as possible about observing accurately.

2. Be cautious about jumping to conclusions on the basis of one rating. In order to get fairly valid results it is considered necessary to obtain the judgments of at least three or more independent ratings.[11]

3. If several traits are to be rated, rate only one for all pupils before going to the next. This procedure helps to reduce the "halo effect" and make the results more objective.

4. Check your judgments as a rater with the judgments of several others who have all rated the same group of pupils. Do this with several different rating scales. Find out in this way whether you tend to rate pupils too high, too low, or whether you tend to avoid extremely high or low ratings altogether. Use your finding to improve your methods.

5. Be aware of the following facts. Hahn and MacLean[12] state that research findings have shown them to be true.

　　a. Raters tend to rate their own sex high on desirable traits and low on undesirable ones.

　　b. Men are more lenient raters than women.

　　c. Two ratings by the same rater are no more valid than one.

　　d. Parents usually overrate their children, but tend to underrate superior children.

[11] Harold O. Rugg, "Is the Rating of Human Character Possible?" *Journal of Educational Psychology,* 13 (February 1922), p. 87.

[12] Milton E. Hahn and Malcolm S. MacLean, *General Clinical Counseling in Educational Institutions* (New York: McGraw-Hill Book Co., Inc., 1950), p. 163.

e. Self-ratings tend to be high on desirable traits and low on undesirable ones.

f. In doing self-ratings, superior people tend to underestimate, and inferior people overestimate, themselves. Inferior people are less accurate in their self-ratings.

Limitations. The detailed limitations of rating scales are all implied in the list of suggestions above. In general, limitations tend to cluster around the same errors of observation which have been noted previously. Limitations pertaining to rating scales themselves include: scales prepared by individuals are generally not as good as those prepared by groups of teachers; items are frequently not clearly defined; frequently those who judge are not competent to judge some of the items included; many raters tend to rate too high, too low, or to avoid extreme ratings altogether.

Other Observational Techniques

Casual, unrecorded observations. This is the type of observation which is most commonly used by teachers. When a teacher observes a child having trouble with a problem, she gives him help. If she sees that he is unhappy socially, she tries to do something about it. Hundreds of observations of similar nature take place for every teacher daily. From a scientific standpoint, this type of observation is not considered to be very valid or reliable. Too frequently it results in only vague impressions. Teachers often are at a loss to give specific examples of behavior to illustrate generalizations they have made about a child. It would be neither possible nor desirable to do away with this type of observation because it is of great value if action follows promptly. However, because of its limitations, it must be supplemented with the organized techniques described in the preceding sections of this chapter.

Situational observations. There are two types of techniques which involve the use of observation in special situations. One type, commonly used, occurs when a teacher observes the behavior of pupils in various kinds of normal situations at school—type of behavior exhibited in arithmetic class, in art class, on the playground, and so on. Although this type of observation has been used for many years, it has not specifically been labeled or classified as a "situation" technique.

The other type of situational observation is one in which the situation has been "rigged" or artificially set up as a testing device to observe pupil behavior in a special type of situation. A well-controlled, standardized "situational-test" of this type was used by the U.S. Office of Strategic Services during World War II.[13] The OSS used it to observe officer candidates in frustrating or "stress" situations as a screening device. This technique may deserve some experimentation at the public school level. It is quite likely, however, that any such adaptation to school use would have to be limited to those who do research projects.

Motion pictures, television, stenographic reports, and tape recordings. Each of these techniques has been used to some extent in observing pupil behavior. Usage has been confined for the most part, however, to child study clinics and research projects. None of these, except tape recordings, is really adaptable for use by the classroom teacher. Tape recordings are particularly well suited in language arts activities as a pupil self-evaluation device.

------

[13] For further details in summary form see Robert L. Thorndike and Elizabeth Hagen, *Measurement and Evaluation in Psychology and Education* (London: John Wiley & Sons, Ltd., 1955), pp. 305–11.

CHAPTER III

Informal
Self-Expression Techniques

Any techniques which utilize structured situations for obtaining responses of pupils for purposes of evaluation are classified here as self-expression techniques. *Informal* self-expression techniques are those which do not lend themselves well to precise measurement or standardization of responses as do tests and some projective techniques.

The number and variety of informal self-expression techniques which might be used by teachers is almost limitless since pupils may be encouraged to express themselves in so many different ways in so many different situations. Only those most commonly used are described here: autobiographies, compositions, oral expression, permissive discussion, diaries, questionnaires, personal data blanks, interviews, dramatic play, role-playing (psychodrama, sociodrama), and self-evaluation techniques.

Many of the purposes, advantages, and disadvantages of all of these techniques are similar. To avoid repeating these for each technique, the following generalizations may be made about all of them.

Purposes and advantages

1. The chief purpose of these informal techniques, as with all evaluative techniques, is to gain clues or insights into causes of pupil behavior.

2. Their unique purpose is to gather information about pupils' attitudes, feelings, and values that is difficult to obtain by the use of observation or testing methods.

3. Some of these techniques are especially good for getting pupils to express things of a personal nature about themselves which they would be reticent to reveal through direct questions.

4. The information obtained is useful as supplementary data which

teachers and counselors may use to help verify or discount other more objective data.

5. The information obtained is useful as a basis for conferences with pupils and their parents.

6. Most of these techniques are suited to use with groups, making it possible to gather a considerable amount of information in a short time.

7. Sometimes self-expression techniques serve a purpose other than that of evaluation. For some children, expressing themselves freely about their problems or worries acts as a catharsis, relieving them of pent-up emotional tensions.

Disadvantages and cautions

1. Many data obtained by these techniques are not very valid and reliable by themselves. Used as corroborative data with the results from more objective measurement they become more valuable. Validity and reliability are also improved if information from several of the informal self-expression or observation techniques is pooled.

2. It is difficult, if not impossible, to interpret self-expressive data without the interpreter projecting his own background of experience into his interpretation.

3. Many data resulting from the use of these techniques are difficult to interpret in the absence of special training. Even psychologists with special training are cautious in jumping to conclusions on the basis of isolated bits of information.

4. Teachers without special training in psychology should use these techniques only if they are thoroughly aware of the limitations suggested above.

Autobiographies

The autobiography is a pupil's own story of his life. It may on occasion be highly objective, but it is more probable that many statements in it will depart from the facts, reflecting instead the pupil's attitudes and feelings. The fact that certain attitudes or feelings do exist gives clues to understanding the pupil better, but the teacher should be aware that the pupil may be unconsciously slanting his story to make himself appear to be better than he really is.

Types. The various forms of pupil autobiographies which teachers use may be grouped into three types. First, many teachers merely ask the pupils to write the stories of their lives in any way they wish. This type is desirable because the freedom of expression allowed reveals the things which pupils themselves consider most important in their lives. There is an important disadvantage, however, to the use of this type. Pupils may forget many important aspects of their life stories. This is a more serious disadvantage with elementary school pupils.

It is because of this disadvantage that most teachers use the second type, the structured autobiography. To keep as much freedom of expression as possible, an advantage of the first type, it is considered better practice to include only major areas in the outline pupils are given to follow. If many details are included, the value of free expression is lost and the autobiography tends to change character and become a questionnaire or personal data sheet. Almy has suggested a few items which may be used:[1]

> Before I Started to School
> When I First Went to School
> School Experiences
> Summer Vacations
> The Most Interesting Thing so Far
> Troubles I Have Had
> Personal Interests
> Companions
> Future Plans

The third type of autobiography is the *partial* or *separate topic* type. Some teachers ask pupils to write, for example, only the story of their school experiences. At some later date they may ask them to write about their most interesting experiences. They may stop here, or they may have a series of papers written periodically throughout the school year until they have the equivalent of a complete autobiography when all the papers are put together.

Suggestions for using autobiographies

1. So that pupils will feel free in expressing themselves, the teacher must motivate them to write their autobiographies. A part of this motivation must include a feeling of rapport between teacher and pupils. If such feelings of mutual trust exist, pupils will write of their feelings when the teacher assures them that their papers will be kept confidential.

2. If pupils have never written an autobiography before, they will need some help. The teacher may read some excerpts from good auto-

---

[1] Millie Almy, *Ways of Studying Children* (New York: Bureau of Publications, Teachers College, Columbia University, 1959), pp. 140–41.

biographies or have the pupils read some. She will probably need to discuss the problem of content with them and perhaps even suggest a few of the main topics they may want to include in their stories.

3. Give pupils several days in which to do their writing if you expect to get more than a sketchy recital of facts. On the other hand, if too much time is allowed, spontaneity of response is reduced for those pupils who have discussed the matter at home.

4. Pupils get bored by having to write their life stories nearly every year. Yet it may be desirable to have them write as many as three during their school years to give both pupils and teachers a picture of changes which have occurred. The school staff should plan the grade levels at which they are to be written, perhaps during the fifth, eighth, and eleventh grades. Classroom teachers, counselors, English teachers, or homeroom teachers may be assigned this responsibility.

5. Autobiographies are a good source of information about new pupils, but it is a good idea to postpone assigning them for a few weeks until the pupils become oriented to their new school situation and gain rapport with the teacher.

6. This technique has some value for use with elementary school pupils, but it is more valuable at the secondary school level because adolescents tend to be more introspective.[2]

7. If free expression of feelings and attitudes is the desired result, do not, for this assignment, place emphasis upon such mechanical aspects of the writing as construction of sentences, spelling, and punctuation.

Example of an autobiography. The following example is an autobiography written by a boy who was a high school senior:[3]

> I was born August 15, 1930 at the hospital in _____. I was the first and only child of our family. My parents had not been married long when I was born.
>
> Both of my parents worked during the time before I went to school. I had several baby sitters who stayed with me. Most of them were old ladies who were bossy and wouldn't let me do the things other children were doing. One time my mother lost her job and stayed home with me for about 6 months.
>
> I started school at _____. It was a long way to walk and I didn't know any of the kids in my grade. Kindergarten was lots of fun because there were lots of toys to play with even though I didn't know anyone. At the end of the year we moved to another

---

[2] G. W. Allport, *The Use of Personal Documents in Psychological Science* (New York: Social Science Research Council, 1942), p. 80.

[3] Clifford P. Froehlich and Kenneth B. Hoyt, *Guidance Testing* (Chicago: Science Research Associates, Inc., 1959), pp. 354–55.

part of town so I had to go to another school. The teacher was another old lady which none of the kids like. This was the only year I had trouble in school, all of the rest of the time school was easy for me. We moved real often during my grade school so most of the time I got new teachers and new kids in my classes.

When I was in junior high school we moved to a house out in the country. I like the country to live in because there are so many things you can do by yourself. We had a river by our place where you could go fishing and swimming and sometimes my mother would let me go hunting. While we lived there my dad had an old car which went bad, the rear end went out of it and he was going to sell it for junk but finally he let me have it. Most of my spare time I work with the motor to see if I can get it to run better. I have taken it apart three times. My uncle says if I want to be a mechanic it would sure help to know where all the pieces go, I even take the wheels off and learn the parts and how they work on the breaks. Sometimes I go downtown to the garage, and watch the mechanics work on motors.

When I was in the eighth grade my parents got a divorce so now I live with my mother. Sometimes on weekends my mother tells me to go stay with my father. My mother is married again, her husband told me he would buy me a car and gun but dad said he would buy a car for me if I would pay him back. I work whenever I can find a job, I only owe $126.

I have gone to all of high schools here. This place is better in some ways than other schools. It has more men teachers and they are young. They seem to know more about what boys like. I like the shop teacher because he knows a lot about mechanics. We don't have a very good music department they have their pets who get to do all the things.

It seems like all they want you to do here is study, we don't ever have any fun. I wanted to play intramural basketball but no one asked me to be on a team. I think they should assign each student to a team then all of the kids would get to play.

Not to many things around here I like. I probably would be better off to go through high school but don't see how it will help me much.

A summary of a few major insights obtained from this autobiography by the counselor who worked with this boy may serve as an example of some of the worthwhile information a teacher might gain from such material: The boy gave the general impression that he was not happy with his life. He indicated resentment of having to move so many times, of having to be with baby-sitters so much, and of missing out on childhood activities in which other children were permitted to engage. He may have felt that his parents had not really wanted him because he stated that his parents had not been married long when he was born. The boy does not have pleasant relationships with his peers, as evidenced by his statement that he liked living in the country because there were so many things he could do by himself. He evidently attributes his lack of school success to the fact that he had to change schools so often. There is some evidence that he does not like women teachers, and this may stem from a dislike of his mother.

Compositions

Pupils often reveal personal feelings and attitudes toward others in stories or themes they write as assignments in English classes. Such autobiographical information may be inserted in a theme on almost any subject. These stray bits of personal information may help the teacher understand pupils better. There are, however, several special composition techniques a teacher may use if she is purposefully seeking personal data.

First, the autobiography has been described in the preceding section. Second, "open questions," as topics for compositions, may be used effectively to get free expression from pupils. Examples of titles are "If I Had Three Wishes," "What Makes Me Angry," and "What Worries Me."[4] Third, "open question" descriptions of other people may be used as the subjects for themes. For example, pupils may write about "My Favorite Teacher," "My Best Friend," or "The Most Friendly Person I Have Ever Known." Some children find it easier to express themselves freely about others than about themselves, but in commenting about others they indirectly reveal their own feelings. Fourth and fifth, unfinished stories and incomplete sentences are discussed in the chapter on projective techniques. Sixth, compositions based upon pupils' reactions to pictures may reveal pupils' attitudes about the situations portrayed. Pictures on magazine covers are often good for this purpose.

---

[4] For detailed suggestions about the use of open questions, see Hilda Taba, Elizabeth H. Brady, John T. Robinson, and William E. Vickery, *Diagnosing Human Relations Needs* (Washington, D.C.: American Council on Education, 1951).

Oral Expression
and Permissive Discussion

Teachers may obtain personal information from pupils by letting them give talks on some of the same topics as those suggested for written compositions. This technique is a good one to use with primary grade pupils who have not yet developed their writing skills or with older pupils who express themselves better orally than they do in writing. However, the technique has two disadvantages. First, it is much more time-consuming. Second, pupils will not be as free about making personal statements orally in front of their classmates as they would in writing. Some topics may be so personal that the teacher would have to listen to each child individually if she expected to get very much free expression.

Oral expression may also be obtained through permissive discussions. A teacher of any subject often finds topics which are of interest to many of her pupils. If she allows them to feel free to say what they think (within the realm of propriety), she will gain insight about their feelings and attitudes. This technique may take the form of teacher-led, panel, or pupil-led discussions.

Diaries

An excellent definition of the diary has been furnished by Strang: "A diary might be described as an autobiography written concurrently with experience rather than in retrospect."[5] The diary is not very objective, but it is an improvement in one respect over the autobiography because the record of events is made soon after they occur.

The unique purpose served by the diary is that of a supplementary technique which may help reveal personal-social problems of pupils which have not been discovered by the use of other evaluation techniques. It is particularly useful for gathering data about the interests, problems, attitudes, and social relationships of pupils in their out-of-school activities.

Some teachers ask pupils to keep a diary record of any events they wish to record, listing the time, place, and companions who

---

[5] Ruth Strang, *Counseling Techniques in College and Secondary School* (New York: Harper & Brothers, 1937), p. 118.

were with them when the events described took place. The use of an unstructured type of diary such as this permits the teacher to obtain clues for understanding the pupil through his selection of events to record. Others feel that the diary becomes a more objective instrument if pupils are requested to record descriptions of selected events only. This technique is called the *controlled diary*. Using this method, the teacher would ask pupils, for example, to keep a record of the time they spend watching TV for one week, or a record of time devoted to play or study, or a record of only those things which upset them or please them. This type of diary is often called a "log" or a "time schedule."

Several suggestions and cautions should be kept in mind if diaries are used. First, the teacher should let the pupils know what she wants the information for and who will have access to it. Second, keep in mind that pupils have many individual motives in writing the things they do. Some pupils may engage in fantasy and describe events as they would like them to be. Others may exaggerate unacceptable behavior to get more attention from the teacher. Third, there is some danger that pupils may become too introspective if they are required to spend an undue amount of time preparing diary records.

Questionnaires

A questionnaire is a structured paper-and-pencil group interview in which the questions used are usually restricted to one small area of information.

One way of classifying questionnaires is according to their form or structure. Some are lists of open-end questions with enough space between questions to encourage essay responses. Others, similar in nature, allow room for short answers—phrases or short sentences. A second general form, with many variations, is that in which the responses are limited. Some of those commonly used are the Multiple-choice, Yes-No, and Agree-Undecided-Disagree types of response. A third form, often called a questionnaire, is that in which lists of items (not questions) are to be checked or rated. The authors classify this type as a check list, inventory, or rating scale rather than as a questionnaire.

Another way to classify questionnaires is either as published or as teacher-made. Most of the published questionnaires are called personality tests, personality inventories, or problem check lists. The results obtained from them, in terms of total or partial scores, have never proved to be highly valid. However, they have been valuable to teachers and counselors who have studied the responses to individual questions. Teacher-made questionnaires, less well-constructed than the published ones, are more valuable to teachers because they can be put together in a hurry to serve so many immediate and specific purposes.

A third way questionnaires may be classified is by the type of information they seek to obtain from pupils. Some of the information sought is factual in nature, such as the information requested on personal data blanks (name, address, age, health data, and so forth) or the answers to such questions as "What TV programs do you like best?" and "How many books did you read this month?" The other type of information is that which is more subjective in nature. Common questionnaires in this category are attitude, interest, problem, and personality questionnaires. Those which request factual information are more valid; nevertheless, those which are used to gather personality information are very helpful, especially to the teacher, who can view the results in the light of other kinds of evaluation data.

There are countless uses for questionnaires in the classroom. In general, they are used to gather factual information from pupils about themselves and to get expressions of opinion from them about their interests, feelings, and attitudes. The information collected is useful in helping teachers understand the behavior of pupils, as well as guiding teachers and administrators in making curriculum decisions. The questionnaires can be constructed to reveal the common interests and needs of the pupils. The results can be used by the teacher to do a better job of planning teaching units and by the administrator to plan a better school program. Second, questionnaires can measure the degree of achievement of behavior changes which are part of the objectives of the school. For example, an objective of a health unit on "Care of the Teeth" may be to get pupils to brush their teeth regularly. An achievement test on subject matter will not evaluate changes of behavior, but the use of a questionnaire can obtain this type of information without resembling a testing situation. Third, questionnaires may be used to elicit the opinions of pupils about the values or weaknesses of a particular unit of work, a whole course, or the whole program of the school.

Since questionnaires are used so extensively by teachers, an awareness of their limitations may help them be used more effectively. The following limitations are most common: Questionnaires have been criticized as not being valid—this is not as true of those which ask for factual information as it is of those which ask for opinions; many times questions are not clearly understood; some pupils consciously or unconsciously make those responses which will please the teacher; some pupils may not take the questions seriously; a limited-choice type of question may not include the exact response of the pupil; open-end questions which obtain free expression are less objective and difficult to tabulate; and on those questionnaires which ask for factual data young children will need help from their parents. Many of these limitations may be offset to some extent if the teacher will carefully explain the meanings and purposes of the questions.

In view of the limitations of questionnaires, one might wonder why they are used so much. The most powerful advantage is that they make it possible to collect a large amount of information from many pupils in a short time. Other advantages are: They are helpful and a time-saver when used preceding a pupil interview; teacher-made questionnaires are easily adapted to immediate and specific classroom needs of all kinds; they may substitute for an overt display of opinion (for example, a show of hands) in those cases where the teacher does not want pupils to be led by the responses of others; and they may make it easier for pupils to respond to some types of personal information without embarrassment than would personal interviews.

Teachers who want to construct questionnaires for their own classroom use need observe only a few simple rules. They should clearly define the purposes they have in mind and then construct only relevant questions. The questions should be simple and the vocabulary easy to understand. Questions should be numbered and grouped by both the type of question (essay, true-false, and so on) and by the type of information being sought. If the questions used are multiple-choice, be sure that extra spaces are included for the pupil to add responses of his own in case the choices offered are not applicable.

Those who wish to construct more perfect instruments for research purposes must observe more stringent rules. This is necessary if the results must be easy to tabulate or if a good percentage of returns must be obtained from mailed questionnaires. For helpful, detailed rules for this purpose, see Nixon.[6]

To administer a questionnaire most successfully, a few suggestions may prove helpful. The physical conditions of the classroom, such as lighting, heating, ventilation, and so forth, should be good. Some motivation is considered to be necessary. A frank and clear explanation by the teacher of the uses to be made of the information is generally thought to be sufficient motivation, especially if there is good rapport between teacher and pupils. If such a condition exists, the pupils will be easily convinced that their answers will be kept confidential and they will feel free to express themselves fully and honestly. Some people think that anonymity of response results in freer expression; others are doubtful of its value. The latter argue that if the atmosphere of the room is a permissive one, responses will be truthful even if signatures are required; if the atmosphere is filled with distrust, responses will not be honest in either case. Finally, questions which are not clear should be explained. If some pupils have reading difficulties which might lessen their comprehension, some or all questions should be read to them. This will be especially true of primary grade pupils.

Personal Data Blanks

The personal data blank is merely a questionnaire which requests personal data information from pupils. Its customary use is to collect background information about the pupils upon their entrance to school and at the beginning of each school year thereafter. Since this information is usually placed on the cumulative record form, the personal data blank should be constructed to follow the pattern of items on this form (see suggested list of items on pp. 103–104). The data requested by most schools fall in these areas: personal identification, family and home information, health history, and pupil interests.

---

[6] John E. Nixon, "The Mechanics of Questionnaire Construction," *Journal of Educational Research*, 47 (March 1954), pp. 481–87.

Interviews

The interview has been defined as "a conversation with a purpose" or as "an oral questionnaire." A more thorough definition, and one which is applicable to all types of interviews, is that given by Schwartz and Tiedeman:[7]

> In every case, the interview is an exchange of ideas between two people in a face-to-face relationship carried on for a purpose and constructed, or guided, in some degree, by one of the parties involved.

The concern here is with the teacher-pupil interview in which the teacher is responsible for its direction.

Types. Interviews are usually classified by types according to the method used to conduct the interview. In the *directive* interview, the teacher has predetermined the direction the interview should take and has questions in mind which will achieve his purpose. In the *non-directive* interview, the teacher asks open-end questions to encourage the pupil to take the lead in seeking solutions to the problems being considered. In practice, teachers find it desirable to use a mixture of both of these types, depending upon the nature of the problem involved and the personality of the pupil being interviewed. This type is called the *eclectic* interview. Directive type questions would predominate in those interviews conducted to give or obtain factual information, whereas non-directive questions would be useful if the purpose of the interview were to explore the areas of feelings, attitudes, and opinions.

Purposes. The purposes of teacher-pupil interviews are many. Most of them will be included if they are summarized under four main headings. First, the purpose may be to get acquainted and to establish friendly relations with pupils; second, to give or to obtain factual information. The teacher may want personal data or diagnostic information about a pupil's strengths or weaknesses in a subject (for example, much more can be learned about a pupil's problem-solving difficulties by an oral recital of the steps he takes in solving a few problems than will ever be discovered by the knowledge that he missed five out of twenty problems on a written test). A

---

[7] Alfred Schwartz and Stuart C. Tiedeman, *Evaluating Student Progress in the Secondary School* (New York: Longmans, Green & Co., Inc., 1957), p. 206.

third purpose of the interview is to obtain clues to pupils' feelings and attitudes. Such clues may be obtained both by the verbal responses pupils make and by their behavior during the interview. Finally, the interview is used in counseling pupils.

Advantages

1. The interview may be the only technique adapted to obtaining some kinds of personal data.

2. It is exceedingly flexible in several respects. It permits follow-up questions to pupil responses. It is adaptable to many different purposes and to many situations. For example, its use may range from the informal day-by-day interviews (casual conversations) to the formal, structured interview.

3. It permits the teacher to observe pupil behavior while responding to questions, which makes possible a better interpretation of the "whole" situation than would the questionnaire.

4. The interview may yield factual data and, at the same time, result in new learning or have therapeutic values for the pupil.

5. It is an exceedingly good technique for discovering *causes* of behavior. For this reason many counselors like to use the clues obtained from questionnaires as the basis for an interview.

6. It can be used to force the pupil to assume some initiative for thinking through his own problems.

Limitations

1. The interview is time-consuming.

2. It is by nature a very subjective technique. To guard against improper interpretation, the data should be used only as a supplement to more objective information.

3. Data obtained by means of the interview may be false or inaccurate. It frequently happens that the pupils who need the most help are the ones who are either least willing or least capable of giving true and accurate information.

4. The formal interview is an artificial situation for the pupil, and therefore his behavior during the interview may not be typical. This is not a limitation of the informal interview.

Suggestions for conducting interviews. Teachers who wish to learn how to conduct interviews could be very easily confused by a long list of detailed suggestions. Therefore, an attempt has been made to limit the list to the most important principles.

1. Rapport with the pupil should be established before going any

further. If this cannot be accomplished, the results of the interview will be negligible.

2. The purposes of the interview must be explained.

3. These purposes should then be carried out. Questions or brief notes should be prepared if they are necessary as a guide.

4. The interviewer will undoubtedly learn more if he listens more than he talks.

5. If the pupil gets too far off the subject for too long, a gracious way to bring him back should be found.

6. At the close of the interview the pupil should be encouraged to summarize (with guidance, if necessary) the major results of the interview.

7. Some way should be found to insure that the pupil leaves with pleasant feelings. The best way to insure this, of course, is to have him feel that he has been helped during the interview.

8. A written summary of the interview should be made immediately after it is over. Since many points brought out in interviews are forgotten if notes are not made at the time, it is desirable to take very brief notes unless it appears that a pupil will become nervous by this practice. The report should be filed in the pupil's cumulative record folder.

Parent conferences and home visits.[8] Interviews with parents are a source of information which teachers find valuable for assessing pupil behavior. They are also excellent for the teacher to use in imparting information about the child to the parent. Since most parent interviews are scheduled to achieve this two-way communication, the term "conference" usually replaces "interview."

Most of the general principles for conducting interviews with pupils are applicable to teacher-parent conferences. There are a few additional suggestions which should be noted:

1. The problem of becoming acquainted and of establishing rapport will require more attention for a parent conference.

2. The teacher will need to adjust her attitude toward the parent in view of the fact that the parent is a peer and is the one who is the final authority in any decisions made about the pupil.

3. Parents of problem children may have problems of their own which cause them to behave defensively; therefore, the teacher needs to be unusually tactful.

---

[8] For more details about parent conferences, see Katherine E. D'Evelyn, *Individual Parent-Teacher Conferences* (New York: Bureau of Publications, Teachers College, Columbia University, 1945).

4. Some system of released time for the teacher should be devised so that she will be relaxed and free from teaching duties during the conference.

5. The teacher should try to have the parent take the initiative for suggesting causes of behavior and plans of action. She should restrain the great temptation to give advice.

6. Arguments should be avoided. They usually wreck any rapport which has been established and make it impossible to arrive at satisfactory solutions of the problems.

What type of information can the teacher expect to obtain from conferences with parents? The general types are listed here. See Almy[9] for specific examples.

1. Details about the pupil's home environment.

2. Background information about past experiences of the pupil, including items of health history not already known.

3. Expectations or goals parents seem to have in mind for their child.

4. Parental methods of discipline.

5. The degree of understanding of the child which the parent exhibits (his strengths and weaknesses).

6. The attitudes which the parents have toward the school.

The *home visit* is a special type of parent conference. It is a valuable technique for establishing friendly relationships with parents and for gaining insights about the physical environment of pupils. There are three main limitations. Home visits are time-consuming, some parents do not want them, and distractions are often so great (other children present) that it is difficult to have a relaxed conference. If the purpose of the visit is confined to getting acquainted, this third limitation is not important.

Dramatic Play

Young children through the ages have loved to "play house," to pretend and act out the role of mother, father, teacher, or doctor. This is dramatic play or unstructured role-playing. It is the free play of children in which the children spontaneously dramatize roles of people important in their lives, projecting their impressions of the behavior of these people as they have seen them in their own environment.

---

[9] Almy, *op. cit.*, pp. 174–79.

Since much of this play activity is simply imitative of situations the children have observed, it is, in itself, valuable information for the teacher about the pupils' home backgrounds. By observing their play activities she will discover that certain pupils have widely different backgrounds of experience. This information will indicate some of the experiences her pupils need for the formation of new concepts or the alteration of some old ones.

The teacher will also discover, however, that children's unstructured role-playing is more than imitation. She will find that much of the play cannot be taken at "face value" because, by its nature, it is a projection of children's impressions and feelings about the situations they reconstruct. Interpretation of their play is complicated by the necessity of deciding, first, whether the specific behavior was imitative or a projection of the child's feelings, and second, what motive prompted the playing of the role in the first place. Almy gives a good example to illustrate this second source of difficulty:[10]

> The care a little girl lavishes on her doll may represent the love she has felt, but it sometimes symbolizes the cuddling for which she longs. The "spanking" a small boy in his role of "father" administers to his "little boy" may reflect a punishment he has actually received or merely his perception of his father in a disapproving mood. The child who plays "doctor" and assures his "patient" that "this won't hurt you" may himself have been either a brave or a timorous patient.

Proper interpretation of clues of this type requires that the teacher have excellent psychological insight and training, does not jump to conclusions, and bases her judgment on many observations instead of one.

Role-Playing

Role-playing is a broad term for those techniques which involve pupils in spontaneously dramatizing the roles of various people in situations which are important to them as individuals or as groups. These techniques are dramatic play (described in the preceding section) and psychodrama. Dramatic play is unstructured role-playing, whereas psychodrama is structured or planned.

There are three types of psychodramatic experiences—personal,

---

[10] *Ibid.*, p. 152.

interpersonal, and societal. The societal type of psychodrama also has been termed "sociodrama."[11]

The personal type of psychodrama is that which involves a problem of an individual pupil.

> *Example:* A sixth grade boy has been elected to be room "host" for the next month and has expressed fear of it because he does not feel comfortable with it. Different children volunteer to be "on stage" with him to assume roles of men, women, and children while he plays out the job of being "host."

The interpersonal type is that which involves a problem that two or more pupils have in common.

> *Example:* Three fifth grade boys have the same problem indicated above. They role-play introductions among themselves before the rest of the class, and class members take turns assuming roles of various visistors who might come.

The societal (or sociodrama) type is that which presents a problem to the class as a whole.[12]

> *Example:* The fifth grade boys simply could not enter the room without scuffling and shoving each other. It was partly in fun and partly in earnest. However, it was annoying their classmates as well as the teacher. They had role-played many other situations, and the children finally suggested tackling the problem Joe and Harvey hadn't been able to solve. The two boys watched while others played their roles and those of the teacher and their classmates. In the third enactment, the girl playing teacher said, "Boys and girls, this isn't getting us anywhere. We'd better ask the principal to help us." A boy became Mr. Richardson and entered the scene. "What door do you use in this room?" he asked. The children told him they always came in the back door after playing. "Well," said the ten-year-old principal, "from now on, maybe it would work if Joe would always come in the front door and Harvey come in the back door." Everyone had a good laugh, and the boys agreed to the plan.

The three purposes of psychodramas—diagnosis, therapy, and

---

[11] The classification system used here has followed that given by Ronald B. Levy, "Psychodrama and the Philosophy of Cultural Education," in *Psychodrama and Sociodrama in American Education,* ed. Robert B. Haas (New York: Beacon House, Inc., 1949), pp. 225–34.

[12] Hildred Nichols and Lois Williams, *Learning about Role-Playing for Children and Teachers* (Washington, D.C.: Association for Childhood Education International, 1960), pp. 32–33.

education—may be present singly or in combination in each of the types mentioned above. Brief mention of the therapeutic and educational purposes of psychodrama is made in the following paragraphs only because of this mingling of purposes in all role-playing situations. The concern of this monograph is with the diagnostic or evaluative purpose only, but evaluation of pupil behavior is possible in those role-playing situations in which the main purpose is either therapy or education.

Psychodramas staged for diagnostic purposes attempt to view the degree of proficiency of a skill or the nature of concepts the pupils hold about almost any new unit the class is ready to begin.

> *Examples:* To diagnose concepts held by pupils before or after they study the Civil War, let pupils take turns role-playing conversations of either Northerners or Southerners about the slavery question. To diagnose the degree of proficiency of the skill of making change in arithmetic class before or after studying it, let pupils take turns being customer and clerk in a variety of change-making situations.

Psychodramas staged for therapeutic purposes attempt to bring about in individual pupils or in groups better adjustment to problems which are frustrating them.

> *Example:* A new pupil in school is having a tough time finding new friends. The teacher or some pupils see the unhappiness in this newcomer and suggest to the class that they role-play the problem of changing schools. During the role-playing several pupils show that they, too, have had similar troubles. The new pupil's spirits are bolstered by the mere fact that others have had the same problem, and the class members change some attitudes toward their new classmate.

Psychodramas staged for educational purposes are usually aimed at teaching pupils how to behave in a new situation or how to perform a skill.

> *Examples:* Teach pupils how to behave in a new situation by role-playing the approaching school "inoculation day"; that first day you are sick and have to have a substitute teacher come in; the occasion when a new pupil may arrive. Practice skills by role-playing introductions; asking for a date; telephoning; applying for a job.

The evaluative purposes of role-playing, in addition to the two mentioned earlier (skill and concept evaluation), are as follows:

1. To find clues which may help explain behavior of pupils (home experiences, attitudes, fears, needs, prejudices, desires, and so forth).

2. To check on validity of other data.

3. To give the pupil an opportunity to evaluate himself by letting him see how he compares with classmates in such areas as those mentioned in 1 above.

The methods of inaugurating and conducting role-playing are very important because success or failure with this technique hinges almost entirely on the way the activity is directed. The following list is a summary of the most important suggestions.[13] (Refer to the example given for the societal type of psychodrama, page 41, for a better understanding of these suggestions.)

1. A role-playing situation which fits one of the types and purposes mentioned above should be selected. Pupils should be enthusiastically motivated to explore the problem suggested, or the idea should be dropped. After pupils have learned the technique, they themselves will often suggest problems of their own.

2. Pupils should be encouraged to volunteer for the roles to be played. They should *never* be embarrassed by being forced to take part.

3. Pupils should thoroughly discuss the situation and the roles to be portrayed. They must understand the details of the situation and feel as if they "know" the characters involved. This preliminary or "warming up" process will prepare them emotionally to lose their own identities as they spontaneously play the roles of others.

4. The pupils should act out the situation or problem spontaneously —no rehearsals. The teacher must make no attempts to direct the action, even though the performance may be inadequate in every respect.

5. After the performance the actors should comment upon their own portrayal of the situation; then the other pupils may add their remarks. If the teacher takes part in the discussion, she should not make any judgment about the solution reached being "right" or "wrong." If there is *one* "right" solution which she intends to tell them about anyway, she should not waste their time searching for a solution (insisting on her solution will cause pupils to try to guess what she wants when, at a later date, role-playing is tried again).

6. Several other groups of volunteers should give their interpretations of the roles and follow each performance with discussion.

---

[13] There are many important aspects of role-playing which cannot be included in this monograph. The most practical reference for busy teachers is that by Nichols and Williams, *op. cit.* Also, see Levy, *op. cit.,* and Helen H. Jennings, "Sociodrama as Educative Process," in *Fostering Mental Health in Our Schools* (Washington, D.C.: Yearbook of the Association for Supervision and Curriculum Development, 1950).

7. The teacher's contributions should consist mainly of questions to initiate the discussions, such as "Did John play his part the way you would have done it?" "How did John show that he understood the way Mary felt?"

8. The same cautions that were mentioned at the end of the section on dramatic play apply here.

Self-Evaluation Techniques

In addition to the self-expression techniques described in this chapter which may be adaptable to pupil self-evaluation, several of the observational techniques covered at length in the previous chapter may also be used for this purpose. Rating scales, check lists, and inventories have been used extensively in obtaining self-evaluations in the areas of attitudes, problems, personal and social adjustment, and interests. A number of these techniques have been utilized in making published instruments which evaluate the pupils in these four areas. Some of them are described in Chapters IV through VII of this book. Others may be located in Buros.[14]

---

[14] Oscar K. Buros, ed., *Mental Measurements Yearbooks* (Highland Park, N.J.: The Gryphon Press). The last of the series was the *Fifth Mental Measurement Yearbook,* 1959.

CHAPTER IV

Projective Techniques

The whole field of projective testing is very broad and includes many techniques and procedures such as The Rorschach Test, The Thematic Apperception Test, drawings of the human figure, finger painting, puppetry, play therapy, psychodrama, and word association and sentence completion.

The chief purpose of all these tests and procedures is to stimulate the subjects to reveal themselves, or certain aspects of themselves, so that more accurate psychological assessments may be made. The basic assumption is that through the use of projective methods an individual will reveal particularly those facets of his personality which are unconsciously motivated. Obviously the more any kind of behavior is determined by unconscious factors, the less a person is able to understand or to talk about this behavior regardless of how willing he may be to do so. The main purpose, then, of all projective methods is to set up stimulus situations which will induce individuals to reveal significant trends in ego-defensive mechanisms.

The rationale of projective-type measurements may be better understood when it is pointed out that all of us reveal ourselves to some extent in all our expressive behaviors, such as walking, talking, hand-shaking, handwriting, gestures, and tonal inflections. Everything we do is interrelated with our total personalities and, to some extent, reveals the kind of person involved in the act. Projective-type tests are specialized techniques for inducing a person to reveal himself primarily through verbal and written expressions or through drawings.

Survey of Projective Tests

The particular technique employed to arouse these expressions varies with the test. The Rorschach Test[1] requires the subject to tell what he sees in each of ten ink-blot figures. In using the Thematic

---

[1] Available from The Psychological Corporation of New York City.

Apperception Test (TAT)[2] the testee is presented with twenty pictures containing a large amount of ambiguous content and is asked to construct a story about each picture. A projective-type test which has been studied extensively by Machover[3] simply asks the subject to draw a human figure. Of a similar nature is a testing technique presented by Buck[4] which directs the testee to make a freehand drawing of a house, tree, and person. Bolgar and Fischer[5] have promoted the use of the World Test,[6] an instrument which presents a child with over 200 colored pieces of wood and metal with which he is to construct anything he wishes. Another projective test, Rosenzweig Picture-Frustration Study,[7] directs the subject to respond to a series of pictures, each one of which depicts a human conflict situation. A recently available projective test for use in individual testing of children is the Structured Doll Play Test (SDP) by Lynn.[8]

A clinical-type projective test, especially designed for use with children, has been prepared by the Bellaks.[9] The test materials consist of ten pictures of animal figures in a variety of situations. The theory behind the selection of these figures is that animals are preferred identification figures for children from three to ten years old. The chief objective of the test is to provide greater understanding of a child's interpersonal relationships and his motivations, with special reference to sibling rivalry, parental relationships, aggression, and fears.

Another projective-type instrument is labeled The Story of Jimmy, developed in 1957.[10] This test can be administered to school

2 Available from The Psychological Corporation of New York City.

3 K. Machover, Personality Projection in the Drawing of the Human Figure (Springfield, Illinois: Charles C. Thomas, Publisher, 1949).

4 J. N. Buck, "The H-T-P Test," Journal of Clinical Psychology, 4 (1948), pp. 151–58.

5 H. Bolgar, and L. K. Fischer, "Personality Projection in the World Test," American Journal of Orthopsychiatry, 17 (1947), pp. 117–28.

6 Presented and described in the Journal of Clinical Psychology, 4 (1948), pp. 151–58, 397–405; and 5 (1949), pp. 37–76.

7 S. Rosenzweig, E. E. Fleming, and L. Rosenzweig, "The Children's Form of the Rosenzweig Picture-Frustration Study," Journal of Psychology, 26 (1948), pp. 141–91.

8 Available from Test Developments, Box 8306, Denver, Colorado.

9 L. Bellak and S. S. Bellak, "Children's Apperception Test" (New York: C.P.S. Co., P.O. Box 42, Gracie Station, 1949).

10 Produced by the Institute of Child Study, University of Toronto, Toronto, Canada.

groups. In responding to this scale the pupils check one of five possible solutions to described life-situations. These five alternatives vary from a high degree of "independent security" (feelings of personal security) to a very low degree of "insecurity." In fact, the primary purpose of The Story of Jimmy is to measure varying degrees of security and insecurity in pupils in grades four through eight.

The Story of Jimmy is a good example of a projective test which purports to measure only within a particular personality area which is clearly stated. The concept of security is defined as a "child's willingness to accept consequences for his decisions or behavior." It is assumed that the more secure a child is, the more he is able to face mistakes and failures and to take some form of constructive action. It is, of course, also assumed that each pupil will project himself into the role of Jimmy. Although the data presented in the manual on reliability and validity indicate that this test is still in an exploratory stage, it appears to be a promising scale for teachers to use in their efforts to evaluate a highly significant but elusive aspect of personality. Its chief practical defect at present is a cumbersome procedure for scoring.

The wide range of techniques mentioned above indicates that projective testing is not limited to any one kind of stimulus content. Instead it is a highly flexible kind of testing which can be varied according to age levels, the purposes of the examiner, or the requirements of a particular personality theory. A good statement on the general assumption behind all projective-type testing is given by Morris when he says:

> This general principle may be stated simply as follows: given a stimulus that allows freedom of association, the individual will draw upon his own background of experience, wishes, needs, conflicts, and so on, in organizing and constructing his response insofar as he is willing and able to cooperate in the activity proposed.[11]

Undoubtedly the strongest and most persistent criticism of all forms of projective testing concerns the lack of conclusive data on validity and reliability. Although a large number of research studies

---

[11] Woodrow W. Morris, "Other Projective Methods," Chap. 18, *An Introduction to Projective Techniques,* eds. Harold H. Anderson and Gladys L. Anderson (Englewood Cliffs, N.J.: Prentice-Hall Inc., 1951), p. 518.

are available, such as those reviewed by Garfield,[12] the overall picture is one of low reliability and validity. In spite of this fact many clinical psychologists are confident that the projective techniques are their best tools for gaining insights into the total personality dynamics of the individual.

Although educators could profit in understanding personality dynamics by studying the literature on all forms of projective testing, it seems probable that the kinds of projective data most likely to be utilized in school settings are those coming from (1) finger painting and drawings, (2) creative stories, and (3) sentence completion tests.

Finger Paintings and Drawings

Finger paintings and drawings are excellent projective media because with these materials the subject is free to create his own product. In contrast, in most projective tests, such as the Rorschach and TAT, the testee must react to prearranged stimulus content. The very unstructured behavior of the former is likely to result in greater self-expression and freedom from blocking or resistance, but, however, causes greater difficulty in arriving at standards for interpretation of the finished products. This being true, teachers and counselors who utilize finger paintings and drawings as aids in personality diagnosis must not expect to find a manual which presents easy and sure guides to interpretation. Instead they must become sensitized through study and experience to signs and leads, and they must always relate these kinds of evidence to other sources of knowledge about a particular pupil.

As in other projective methods it is essential that the individual being evaluated be encouraged to talk about his paintings and drawings. When working with an individual pupil it is best to try to have him verbalize while he is working by encouraging him to say aloud what he is making, what the different parts represent to him, and how he feels about the various figures and lines he portrays. If a pupil does not talk about his work while producing it, he should be strongly encouraged to do so after it is finished. This discussion will be most difficult for those students who have deep-seated emo-

---

[12] S. L. Garfield, *Introductory Clinical Psychology* (New York: The Macmillan Company, 1957).

tional conflicts. Also, those who have very limited vocabularies or who are of low intelligence will not be able to verbalize well.

When finger painting and drawings are done on a group basis, as is usually the case in schools, some pupils will be more self-expressive than when their work is observed in an individual setting since they are less aware of being watched and have the stimulation and support of doing the same task as the others. The chief disadvantage is that some pupils may be too much influenced by the creations of the others. This behavior, however, is diagnostic since it often shows overdependency. A child who copies others needs to be encouraged on an individual basis to do work which he can be proud of because it is his own. He needs help in accepting himself and his ideas as being worthy of expression. Paintings and drawings afford a good beginning point for this kind of personality development.

This account is necessarily too brief to present much detailed help to teachers, but a few statements will suggest the possibilities for personality diagnosis which are afforded through finger painting and drawings.

With reference to finger painting, Napoli[13] gives the following interpretations of particular kinds of responses: Lack of neatness is indicative of poor coordination, feelings of guilt, lack of respect for social amenities, or resentment of authority. Reluctance to paint is generally due to unusual timidity, anxiety, or to fearful and guilty attitudes. Obvious displeasure with the finished product often means feeling of inadequacy, fear of criticism, or a sense of shame in regard to what the painting may reveal. Frequent patting movements are typical of children who have received much favorable attention and affection. Scratching is generally a means of showing feelings of defiance and a desire to destroy what is represented by the symbols portrayed. Slapping is indicative of feelings of rejection and of inadequacy. Slow, weak, and poorly directed physical movements generally denote feelings of depression or serious lack of motivation.

In reference to the symbolical significance of particular items in a painting, Napoli gives the following clues: Fences and ladders represent psychological barriers. Heavy circular movements which

---

[13] P. J. Napoli, "Finger Painting," Chap. 14, *An Introduction to Projective Techniques, op. cit.*

the pupil calls "wheels" symbolize feelings of power. Dead animals generally reflect feelings of rejection. Snakes symbolize either enemies or sex problems. Roaring animals typify aggression, especially in older subjects. Crawling monsters are most likely to represent some kind of sex experience or sex preoccupation. An unusual amount of grass may indicate evasiveness, and when the grass is referred to as "hairs" a sexual reference is generally involved.

In regard to the significance of colors, Napoli offers the following leads: A normal use of *blue* indicates security and drive, but an extreme amount denotes impulsive and violent behavior. When this is the only color used by a female it is very likely that she is rejecting her own sexuality. *Green* is frequently used by those individuals who have well-developed but also well-controlled emotions. *Red* is used in fairly large proportions by both sexes under six years of age. In later years a generous use of red by males is usually indicative of female domination or of difficulty in psychosexual identification. Constructive use of *yellow* by a female denotes good social values and good acceptance of males, while a perverted or peculiar use of yellow reflects deceptive traits and is also characteristic of the flirt or coquette. Normal males use yellow sparingly and such use shows good acceptance of females, but an excessive use of yellow generally denotes inadequacy in meeting life situations as a man. When *black* is used in excessive amounts and in a poorly directed manner it denotes the presence of fears, depressive states, and unexplained emotionality. Abnormal use of *brown* represents negative attitudes toward everyday living. Normal use of *purple* denotes good heterosexual adjustments; excessive use of purple reflects depressive feelings with overtones of optimism and confidence.

From their extensive investigations of the personality implications of children's paintings, Alschuler and Hattwick[14] state that color gives the clearest indications of the nature of a child's emotional life, while line and form are useful primarily as revealing the amount of energy that is being expended and how it is being directed. When color and form are considered together, they give clues to the degree

---

14 Rose H. Alschuler, and La Berta Weiss Hattwick, *Painting and Personality— A Study of Young Children,* Vol. I (Chicago: The University of Chicago Press, 1947), p. 14.

of balance which a child has achieved between his impulsive drives and his overt behavior.

Speaking of the significance of different colors for young children, Alschuler and Hattwick agree essentially with the statements of Napoli. These authors classify red, yellow, and orange as warm colors and state that children who use them extensively are generally characterized by free emotional behavior, affectionate relations with others, and also by the kind of self-centered orientation natural for children of the ages studied. Alschuler and Hattwick classify blue, black, green and brown as cool colors. Children who consistently prefer these cool colors are characterized as being highly controlled, overadaptive, critical, assertive, and undemonstrative in relations with others. These children are frequently described by such expressions as: "intellectual interests," "aggressive in contacts," "determined will," "play alone." Home visits produced data to show that the "cool color" children tended as a group to come from homes which exerted an excessive amount of pressure toward control of feelings.[15]

Alschuler and Hattwick point out that as children become more mature, both chronologically and psychologically, their choices of colors for painting are determined more by reality or objective considerations and are, therefore, less indicative of personality adjustments. It should be stressed, however, that large numbers of people retain various aspects of psychological immaturities into adult years, and, consequently, color preferences continue to carry the kind of symbolical implications already described. Obviously much care needs to be exercised to try to determine, in any individual, the extent to which his color preferences are motivated by symbolical as opposed to objective considerations.

A teacher or counselor who uses artistic products as an aspect of personality evaluation should study the literature in this field and should also, if possible, take a graduate course in which this kind of material is covered. The aim should be, not to learn some rules of thumb, but rather to deepen insight and heighten sensitivity to the many subtle ways whereby children and young people reveal themselves through their artistic productions. Extended study interwoven with experience in relating artistic expressions to personality variables will yield increasing rewards in understanding.

---

[15] *Ibid*, p. 18.

One general caution is that one painting or drawing should never be considered alone, as if it were by itself a personality index; rather, attention should be centered on consistency of theme over a period of weeks, during which time a minimum of six or seven samples are available.

Story Completions

As stated in reference to the TAT, it has been shown that the telling of stories in response to a relatively unstructured stimulus has been shown to be a valuable form of personality diagnosis. While only a few school systems have the qualified personnel necessary to use the TAT, teachers can frequently gain some insight into the personal-social problems of pupils by asking them to write original stories or to complete a story from a stated topic. When one topic is given to a whole class, it should be of a fairly general nature, such as "The Story of a Family," "The Story of a Boy" (or Girl), "A Success Story," "A Story of Two Friends," or "A Day at School." It is best not to make a topic very specific, such as "A Story of My Brother" or "A Story About Bob," because such topics are likely to arouse associations in reference to particular individuals rather than stimulate self-projections into the story content.

If a teacher is going to utilize stories as an aid in personality assessment he should collect a series of stories designed for this purpose throughout a semester, probably at least four or five. No standardized or objective scoring exists for the kind of story completions discussed above; therefore, a teacher must rely upon his general knowledge of child development, his experience, and his specific knowledge of psychological motivations to pick up significant themes which offer leads for better understanding of personality. Intellectually bright children are more likely to produce significant stories than are dull pupils. Of course, a teacher should be aware that a story may be simply a highly imaginative product without much direct bearing on the personality dynamics of the writer. This means that story completions should always be evaluated in conjunction with other sources of information about a pupil.

Many teachers have found that they frequently get some very interesting insights into children by asking them to write on such topics as "If I Had Three Wishes," "If I Had a Million Dollars," or

"If I Could Do Just What I Want To Do." In order to illustrate different levels of responses to these kinds of topics, three examples are given below—all of them written by fifth grade pupils.

The first was written by a very normal, reality-orientated boy.

If I Had a Million Dollars

If I had a Million I think I would put $100,000 in the bank and then buy a farm with part of it. Then I would buy live stock for the farm and put some men on it. Then I would buy a good store and work in it and last I would buy a house. Then if I had any money left I would put it in the bank.

The second example was written by a boy who had been characterized since the first grade by serious inability to do his school work (although he is not mentally retarded), by social isolation from the great majority of his classmates, and by numerous forms of escapism such as fantasy and procrastination. His immaturity and his fixation on lower level satisfactions are revealed in the following composition:

The Day I Did What I Wanted To Do

If I had one day that I could do any thing I wanted to do I would sleep until 10:30 then I would play until lunch. For lunch I would eat as much as I could eat. I would eat hotdogs, hamburgers, and chickens. Then I would go out to play again. When supper came I would have the same things as I had for lunch. I would watch the late movie and then I would have a midnight snack.

The third composition given here was written by a girl who had symptoms of mental retreat and emotional isolation from the objective environment. She was socially isolated, did not play with other pupils, never laughed or smiled, and appeared to daydream a lot. She wrote the statement below in response to an English assignment to write on any topic of interest.

I never was very smart like all other children. Everybody they think that I ought to have a strait A card. Daddy and mother or nobody helps me with my lessons and I can't get them without help. It is not any use for me to be treated like a dog, pig, camel, cat, chicken, or horse. I am going to the lumber yard and buy me enough lumber to build a three room house. Have me a little house to myself to play in so I won't be bothered while I get my lessons.

Home investigations revealed that this girl was not pressured to make grades. Furthermore, her academic work was quite satisfactory. Her feelings of failure and of persecution, including her identification with animals and her desire to have her own house, were apparently motivated by her serious inadequacies. This composition made the teacher much more aware of this girl's problems.

Teachers who are alert to the values of written materials as projective media will find many clues, not only to personality trends, but also to sources of academic difficulties in pupils of normal or better intelligence. For example, Monroe[16] in a journal article presents evidence to show that a picture-story test can be very useful in diagnosing some of the inner psychological problems of children who experience persistent learning disabilities. Such diagnostic material is often available to teachers in school systems which have psychological clinics.

Sentence Completions

The use of sentence completions as a form of projective testing is another kind of psychological assessment which can be used in schools. As the name implies, this testing technique requires the testee to respond to a word, or to several words, by making a more complete sentence. Since the stimulus words are usually of a very general nature, the subject has a wide latitude within which to respond; however, since stimulus words *are* presented, a sentence completion test can best be described as semi-structured, as contrasted with the more unstructured Rorschach Test. The basic assumption in reference to sentence completion measurements is that each subject will project various aspects of himself into his completed sentences. The extent to which his responses actually do reflect his attitudes, fears, or desires depends primarily upon his spontaneity and his willingness to cooperate wholeheartedly with the examiner and the test situation. Also, a few emotionally disturbed individuals may find it difficult, if not impossible, to write down the mental content which is aroused in them by some of the stimulus words. When this kind of blocking occurs, there are likely to be numerous omissions, irrelevant responses, and partially com-

---

16 Ruth L. Monroe, "Diagnosis of Learning Disabilities through a Projective Technique," *Journal of Consulting Psychology*, 13 (1949), pp. 390–95.

pleted sentences. The principal thing a teacher should look for in a sentence completion test is the presence of repeated themes or topics.

In her book *The Sentence Completion Method,* Rohde[17] gives a completion test form consisting of sixty-five items. This form was administered to a class of junior high school students, and the teacher examined the papers for leads in understanding his pupils. He found many such leads, as illustrated by the responses to twenty-eight items reproduced below from a girl's paper.

The future looks dull to me.
I suffer from loneliness.
Friends, have I none.
My mother is nice, but doesn't understand me.
There are times when I want to leave home.
My greatest longing is to have friends.
My imagination sometimes runs away with me.
Most boys dislike me.
My clothes are not what I want.
I fear my father.
My greatest trouble is being friendly.
Many of my dreams are terrible.
Secretly I am lonely.
I cannot understand what makes me have no friends
    when I want them.
Most people are friendly to me, if they do not know me.
I am very much afraid of people that I know.
I envy girls who can do what they want to.
When I have friends, I will be happy.
Children are unthinking.
Girls usually are worse than boys.
My greatest ambition is to be in Africa.
My habits are horrible.
I try to get friendly, but I can not.
Love in my life was never there.
I feel hurt when someone insults me.
Often I think of adventure.
No one likes me.
I am ashamed of myself.

These responses made this teacher vividly aware of how much this girl suffered from feelings of inferiority, guilt reactions, and fantasy escapes.

---

[17] A. R. Rohde, *The Sentence Completion Method* (New York: The Ronald Press Company, 1957), pp. 60–61.

Other themes which frequently occur in sentence completion tests among secondary school students are: conflicts with parents, shyness or antagonism toward members of the opposite sex, fears of the future, dislike of school, preoccupation with moral and religious demands, and attitudes of lassitude and indifference.

Although sentence completion data are generally interpreted in clinical settings in reference to unconscious motivations, it is probably safer for school personnel to regard these responses simply as sources of information on the thoughts and feelings of an individual. In the sample responses given above by the junior high school girl, it is apparent that what she wrote was a direct expression of what was in her conscious awareness. However, she may not have been fully aware of the fantasy escape tendencies which seem to be revealed in such sentences as *"My greatest ambition* is to be in Africa" and *"Often I think* of adventure." It would seem to be the best policy, however, for teachers and school counselors not to try to discover hidden motivations in sentence completions, but rather to regard them as rich sources of information on the thoughts, wishes, and desires of their pupils. From her long experience with this means of personality evaluation, Rohde[18] states that although deeper analyses of sentence completion responses can be made by psychologists and psychiatrists, nevertheless, other professional workers, such as teachers and counselors, can make important and valid deductions from this material.

In spite of the semi-unstructured nature of sentence completion responses, several investigations have developed techniques for scoring these kinds of responses and for classifying them into categories. Space in this discussion does not permit an elaboration of these procedures; furthermore, a number of authorities believe that such scoring schemes are premature, cumbersome to manage, and in all instances must depend a lot on the examiner who does the scoring. The interested reader should consult references by Rohde[19] and Rotter and Willerman.[20]

The manual of The Rotter Incomplete Sentences Blank affords a

18 *Ibid.,* p. 67.

19 *Ibid.*

20 J. B. Rotter and B. Willerman, "The Incomplete Sentences Test as a Method of Studying Personality," *Journal of Consulting Psychology,* 11 (1947), pp. 43–48.

good illustration of how the responses to such an instrument can be classified into various categories in order to aid in diagnosis. The categories for classification used by Rotter are: Familial Attitudes, Social and Sexual Attitudes, General Attitudes, and Character Traits. He also presents a procedure for scoring all responses. Although Rotter's materials have been developed particularly for use with college students, they could also be used on the high school level.

Any use of sentence completions in schools should presuppose a serious professional purpose, some psychological training, and at least several years of experience in teaching or counseling. Also such data should not be used in isolation but should be integrated with other sources of knowledge about particular children.

It seems likely that the sentence completion form quoted from Rohde's book offers as good a form as can be had for school use. However, one of the advantages of this kind of personality assessment is its flexibility. When a prepared scoring procedure is not used, an examiner can make up his own items for sentence completions to fit any major purpose he may have.

An example of this kind of "home-made" completion test is given in a journal article by Wilson.[21] She presented forty incomplete sentences to a group of high school students selected by members of the administrative staff as being maladjusted and to a comparable group considered to be well-adjusted. Most of the items had some reference to school situations, such as *If only teachers . . .*, *The rules around here . . .*, *The pupils in this school . . .*, *On examination almost everyone . . . .* The chief purpose of the study was to see if the two groups mentioned above could be distinguished on the basis of the completion responses. The students did not sign their names.

Results showed that on thirteen items there were large differences in the kind of responses given by the two groups under study and practically all of these made reference to school situations. The author considers her data too limited for generalizing, but she is confident that sentence completion responses are a valuable aid in understanding many adolescents. This point was emphasized in the

---

[21] Isabell Wilson, "The Use of a Sentence Completion Test in Differentiating between Well-Adjusted and Mal-Adjusted Secondary School Pupils," *Journal of Consulting Psychology*, 13 (1949), pp. 400–402.

case of one boy in the so-called well-adjusted group. His responses showed clearly that he suffered from several kinds of emotional and social problems, which apparently were not noticed or were underestimated by the administrative officials who selected him as being among the best adjusted students in the school.

Sentence completions may also be constructed as a tool for investigating particular problem areas. This kind of use is illustrated in one study on the nature of aggression.[22] Fifty incomplete statements concerning various aspects of aggressive behavior were constructed and administered to several groups of adolescents. Such statements as the following were used: *When John's mother hit him, he . . . ; The colored kid called him names, so Ricky . . . ; When her mother bawled her out like that, Thelma . . . .*

The basic assumption in this study, as in all others using projective techniques, was that the young people who completed these statements would, through the personality mechanism of projection, reveal their own aggressive attitudes.

Caution Needed in Using
Projective-Type Assessments

Several times in the preceding discussion emphasis was placed on the need for caution in using any kind of information which is assumed to be based on self-projections. In the first place, we cannot be sure that all members of a group are sincerely revealing anything about themselves. A few may not be willing to cooperate with the expectations of the test situation; a few may not be able to express their thoughts or feelings, especially in written form; and a few others may deliberately distort their responses. In the second place there is much controversy among psychologists and psychiatrists in regard to the validity of all forms of projective-type tests, including the Rorschach. It is not possible or desirable in this discussion to consider the details of this controversy; but it is important that teachers and counselors be aware that the valid use of the kind of projective data described in this chapter depends primarily upon the training and skill of the one who handles this information.

Many psychologists who are well aware of the values of projective

---

[22] F. K. Graham, W. A. Charwat, A. S. Honig, and P. C. Weltz, "Aggression as a Function of the Attack and the Attacker," *Journal of Abnormal and Social Psychology,* 46 (1951), pp. 512–20.

methods are also well aware that in spite of a large amount of research the validity of these methods is still inconclusive and unsatisfactory. The personality assessments obtained from projective tests are frequently not in agreement with interview assessments given by clinical psychologists and psychiatrists. As do many other writers in this field, Macfarlane and Tuddenham state at the beginning of their discussion on "Problems in the Validation of Projective Techniques"[23] that despite the unsatisfactory validity of these techniques, nevertheless, on the basis of present research, there is a very general belief among clinicians that these tests are their most useful tools in diagnosis.

In conclusion we may say that teachers and counselors should use projective-type materials for aid in personality assessment, but only when they have taken some courses in these areas, have read fairly extensively on these topics, have resolved that they won't "jump to conclusions," and have other sources of information about their pupils for counterchecking.

---

[23] Chapter 2, *An Introduction to Projective Techniques, op. cit.*

CHAPTER V

Sociometric Techniques

The term sociometry has occurred with increasing frequency in educational literature during the past twenty years. Briefly stated, sociometry is concerned with the measurement of interpersonal preferences among the members of a group in reference to a stated criterion. The whole field of sociometry, however, is multi-dimensional in the sense that it includes not only measurement techniques but also methods and principles to be followed in making groups more effective in pursuit of their goals and more personally satisfying to their members.

Since the chief focus of this discussion is on evaluation techniques, attention will be centered on the value of sociometric data as a source for understanding pupils' personalities. As contrasted with projective techniques, whose aim is to ferret out inner psychological states, the purpose of sociometric methods is to measure each individual's social stimulus value, or in other words, his social worth or personal value as viewed by his group associates. In a more general sense, what is measured is primarily overt group adjustment or acceptability. This kind of assessment is probably more in accord with what is generally thought of as a "good personality" than is the assessment gained either from projective tests or from adult ratings. It cannot be assumed, however, that a sociometric test necessarily measures popularity since much depends upon the particular choice-criterion utilized.

Assumptions

Sociometric measurements are based on several assumptions. One of these is that within any formal organization, such as that existing in a school class, there is an informal organization based on interpersonal attractions and repulsions, and that these informal relationships greatly affect the official functioning of the group, as well as having important personality consequences for each person in the group. Through sociometric testing these informal organizations can be measured and quantitatively described. Another assumption of sociometry is that interpersonal bonds between the members of a group are necessary to good morale and to the normal personality growth of each individual. Man is a social as well as a biological being and, therefore, has basic needs for many associations with others and for reciprocation of positive feelings. If these assumptions are accepted, it naturally follows that an adequate program for personality evaluation of pupils must include data on interpersonal relationships.

Kinds of Sociometric Measurements

Sociometric testing falls into two major categories: (1) The use of choices of specific criteria to serve a particular purpose at a particular time, and (2) questionnaires or rating instruments which measure interpersonal attitudes and feelings but not in respect to a specific, functional-type criterion.

Preferences on specific choice criteria. In utilizing a specific criterion of choice, a teacher asks the pupils to respond to a question which is pertinent to a need in a particular class, homeroom, or club, such as: "Which other pupils in this group (class) would you prefer to work with in arranging for an assembly program?" "Putting on one-act plays?" "Forming discussion groups in social studies?" or "Making up committees for playground and hall duties?"

At other times criteria of a much more personal nature may be used, such as: "Which other pupils would you like to sit by?" or "Which ones do you prefer to have in your play group during play period or noon hour?"

It will be noted that in all the above questions the pupils are not asked to list the names of other children with whom they now associate, work with, or play with, but rather the ones whom they would *like* or *prefer* to have as an associate or partner. Thus what is measured is not necessarily social *facts* but social *aspirations*. This is desirable since the major value of sociometric data lies in their use for changing interpersonal alignments to bring about more satisfying relationships. If a teacher is going to help various pupils in his class, he needs to know not what now exists, but what the pupils would like to have exist so that they could better realize their personal desires.

It will also be noted that all the above questions state criteria which can be acted upon to make changes in the social arrangements of a group. This is the chief value of a specific choice-criterion. It *can* and *should* be used for forming subgroups within a class or a club as soon as the results are tabulated. Moreno,[1] the founder and promoter of sociometry in America, has always insisted that a genuine sociometric test must be one which is specific to a particular situation and which is used as a basis for making changes in accord with the expressed desires of the group members.

Questionnaires and rating instruments. The second major category of sociometric testing, questionnaires and rating instruments, asks the members of a group to indicate their feelings toward each other but not in reference to a specific criterion; nor is there necessarily any expectation that some group changes will result from the testing. Nevertheless, these more generalized kinds of measurements are valuable forms of personal-social assessments. Usually sociometric questionnaires are concerned primarily with measuring interpersonal feelings, as opposed to leadership qualities or desirability as a work-associate.

A typical example of such a questionnaire is found in the Ohio Social Acceptance Scale,[2] which consists of the following six headings: (1) My very, very best friends, (2) My other friends, (3) Not friends, but okay, (4) Don't know them, (5) Don't care for them, (6) Dislike them. Every pupil taking this questionnaire is given a list of the names of all his classmates and is asked to put a number opposite each child's name to indicate his degree of positive, neutral, or negative feelings toward him. This is obviously a very comprehensive measurement since every child responds to every other child in his class. From such data a teacher can be confident that he has a reliable index to the way his pupils regard each other *at the time of the measurements*. In addition, he can have considerable confidence that he has a reliable index to the interpersonal status of his respective pupils over a period of several weeks or even months, since follow-up ratings with the Ohio Social Acceptance Scale and with a similar unpublished scale developed by the writer, designated "How I Feel Toward Others," have shown reliability

---

[1] J. L. Moreno, *Who Shall Survive* (New York: Beacon House, Inc., 1953).

[2] Published by the Division of Elementary Supervision of the State Department of Education, Columbus, Ohio.

coefficients for total scores to average about .78 for periods of several weeks and about .73 for periods of several months.

It is evident from item 6 on the above scale that negative responses are called for. In some sociometric measurements negative or rejecting responses are elicited; in others only positive feelings are asked for. Some writers in the field, as well as some teachers, believe that it is not desirable to ask for negative reactions. They believe that such a procedure arouses unfavorable attitudes in children's minds and may occasionally result in some antagonism to the test situation. In reply to this position it can be stated that sociometric data are much more sharply differentiated when rejecting responses are included; and furthermore, negative interpersonal feelings are a part of normal associations and are not created simply by asking for them in a test situation. However, most of the values of sociometric testing for understanding pupils' needs and social aspirations can be obtained through positive responses alone. Therefore, teachers who believe it is undesirable to ask for rejecting responses need not do so; instead, they can ask only for positive preferences or for varying degrees of acceptance.

Usually, under such testing conditions a few pupils are *isolates* or *fringers* since they receive no choices or only one or two. It cannot be assumed, however, that an isolate is disliked or rejected by his group. It may be that he is just ignored because he is passive, inhibited, mentally retarded, or not well-known. One value of asking for negative evaluations is that definitely rejected children can be distinguished from those who are just ignored. The former must be seen as being in a much more critical social situation than the latter. Rejected children generally need psychological counseling and home adjustments, whereas isolated children need help primarily in making contributions to their groups.

Another instrument which is essentially a sociometric questionnaire is the Syracuse Scales of Social Relations.[3] The major purpose of these scales is to arrive at scores which are indicative of the degree to which each pupil in a class regards all his classmates as sources of satisfaction for his personal-social needs. Each pupil responds to every other pupil on a five point distribution—these five points

---

[3] Manual and test forms for elementary, junior, and senior high school levels developed by E. F. Gardner and G. G. Thompson (New York: Harcourt, Brace & World, Inc., 1959).

consisting of the names of significant persons in the lives of each rater, such as Alice, Neighbor Jones, Uncle Joe, Dan, and Mother. On the elementary school level each child is asked to compare each of his other classmates with the five significant persons whom he has listed at the top of his test form in regard to their value to him as satisfiers of his needs for *succorance* and for *achievement-recognition,* although these terms, as such, are not presented to the pupils. All the categories of needs which are assessed by the Syracuse Scales are based on Murray's discussion of psychological needs.[4]

A major value claimed for the Syracuse Scales is that they measure social relationships of pupils on a broader and presumably a more stable basis than is possible when a reference criterion is limited to a particular group, as is the case with other sociometric measurements. In the manual for these scales the author presents considerable data bearing on the development of norms and in reference to validity and reliability. The normative populations consisted of 395 classes from fifty-two school systems in the northeastern section of the United States. Reliability coefficients with the test-retest procedure on the fifth and sixth grade levels are reported as falling between .67 and .78. A mean validity coefficient of .74 was found between social relations indexes obtained from the Syracuse Scales and the relative degree of *esprit de corps* of fraternities on a large university campus. Also correlations ranging from .32 to .71 were found between scores on several of the need categories assessed by these scales and objective evidences of degree of satisfaction of these needs in elementary school classes.

While it seems certain that Gardner and Thompson have made a distinct contribution in their conception and technique of measuring social relationships, it also seems likely that most teachers would find the Syracuse Scales cumbersome to administer and to use as compared to a specific criterion which has functional value at a particular time. Although the manual cites some evidence to show that the results obtained from these scales are indicative of "morale and effectiveness of individuals in group situations," the authors also state that their scales "in the last analysis . . . merely supply knowledge about the social relationships existing within the classroom or recreational group." They do not directly supply informa-

---

[4] H. A. Murray, *Explorations in Personality* (New York: Oxford University Press, Inc., 1938).

tion which can be used for making social rearrangements within a group such as can be had from a specific and immediately functional criterion.

All forms of sociometric questionnaires are valuable aids in supplying a teacher with a picture of the social structure of his class and also in locating the relative acceptability of each of his pupils within this social structure. Also, such data can be used for research purposes. However, when the chief goal of a teacher is to find the desirability of each pupil as an associate for a particular activity or situation, a specific choice-criterion must be used to fit this objective.

Measures of Reputation

A measure of reputation is not, strictly speaking, a sociometric test since no choices or preferences are given; rather, each member of a group renders judgments in regard to the personal traits or behavior characteristics of his group associates.

An example of a reputation measurement is found in the Ohio Recognition Scale—Who's Who in My Group.[5] Three items from this scale are:

> Do we have any boys and girls in our room who are very even-tempered, who almost never get upset or angry, who are always calm, even when things go wrong? When somebody shouts at them, or even hits them, they don't get excited. They are always cool and level-headed. Who are they?
>
> There are some boys and girls who are always grumbling and making excuses when things don't go right. They can't take a joke and they become angry if anyone criticizes them. They hate to lose and always blame other people if the game isn't going well. Do we have any children like that in our room? Who are they?
>
> There are some children who are strong enough to win fights but they don't pick fights. They don't go around teasing and hitting people. They stop "bullies" from hitting and teasing smaller children. They want everyone to have a square deal. Do we have any children like that? Who are they?

Under each of the eighteen items in this scale, space is left for the writing of names.

Other examples of reputation instruments, together with sug-

[5] Published by the Division of Elementary Supervision of the State Department of Education, Columbus, Ohio.

gestions for their use, are given by Cunningham and Associates[6] and by The Youth Development Series.[7]

Social roles test. Another type of reputation measurement is a social roles test. This kind of instrument differs from the ones described above in that the focus of attention is not on personality traits but on level of performance in various group functions or activities which are quite well-defined and frequently practiced within a particular group. In other words, the purpose of a social roles test in a school situation is to get an assessment from the members of a class or a club concerning which ones are regarded as being the best in various designated group-approved social capacities. It is important to note the emphasis on *social* role or *social* functioning as distinguished from degree of skill or ability. The assumption is that if a teacher wants an assessment of his pupils' degree of skill in any ability area he can best obtain this information from standardized tests or ratings or by examining records, whereas he can obtain an assessment of how the pupils regard each other in their social role functioning by extended observation or by getting responses from the pupils.

Given below is a form used for this type of measurement in a sixth grade class.

What We Can Do Best

Directions: You may put as many names as you wish under any one heading, but you probably will not want to list more than three or four under most of them. If you cannot think of anyone who fits a certain heading do not write any names under it.

1. Which children in the room are best at sharing their experiences with the class?

2. Which ones are best in making good contributions in class discussions?

3. Which ones are the best to play with in a game on the playground or in the gym?

4. Which ones are the best to have as a partner in a table game?

5. Which ones usually have something interesting to talk about outside of class periods?

---

[6] *Understanding Group Behavior of Boys and Girls* (New York: Bureau of Publications, Teachers College, Columbia University, 1951).

[7] "Studying Children and Training Counselors in a Community Program," Series No. 2 (Chicago: The University of Chicago Press, 1953), pp. 135–36.

6. Which ones are best to have in your square for square dancing?

This form was composed for a particular class and could not be used as it is in any other class unless the same social activities are involved. All the items listed above referred to various kinds of social functioning which had been stressed and practiced many times in this class. It will be noticed that items 3, 4, and 6 do not ask which ones are the best in these skills but rather which ones are "best to have as a partner" or "best to play with," or "best to have in your square." Emphasis is thus placed on a child's level of social performance and not simply on level of skill. In other classes such items as the following might be most appropriate: "best to have as leader of a reading group," "best to welcome new pupils," or "best to help you with assignments you missed when you were absent."

Values of social roles testing. What are the values of social role data to a teacher? In the first place, such data afford another kind of measurement of the personal-social adjustments of pupils with which the teacher can compare his own judgments. Furthermore, such data supply a teacher with information in regard to which pupils need to be helped to improve their social functioning in particular areas, and which ones are regarded as not performing in a competent way in *any* social role.

In the sixth grade class mentioned above the teacher found that a few children received over fifteen nominations by classmates as being good in one or more of the roles listed, while a few others received a total of less than five mentions for all the roles combined. These data helped the teacher to see the need of stimulating certain pupils to participate more in various kinds of classroom activities. Furthermore, her attention was called to the fact that a few pupils received a large number of nominations for verbal roles (especially 2 and 5) but very few for any of the roles involving mutual interactions. This discovery led her to make some definite plans for trying to get these highly verbal pupils to engage in and enjoy at least one kind of social skill.

Comparisons with Teacher Judgments

It is sometimes said that sociometric measurements are not necessary because any experienced teacher already knows what these tests reveal. This point has been made the subject of several investigations, notably by Gage, Leavitt, and Stone[8] and by Gronlund.[9] The results of these and other similar studies are consistent in showing that a few teachers are very accurate in assessing the peer acceptance of their pupils prior to sociometric testing, a few are very inaccurate, and most teachers are only moderately successful in predicting the outcome of such measurements. In Gronlund's[10] research, which included forty sixth-grade teachers, he found an average correlation coefficient of .60 between teachers' estimates and sociometric scores.

It should not be surprising that most teachers frequently make erroneous assessments relative to the interpersonal status of at least some of their pupils. A teacher is evaluating from an adult point of view and also from the position of one who is outside the most intimate network within his class. Gronlund[11] found, for example, that most of his teachers overrated those who conformed closely to classroom routines. Conversely they tended to underrate pupils whom they least preferred and who did not adjust readily to classroom activities.

In addition to the fact that teachers are likely to be unduly influenced by their own personal reactions to pupils, many of them do not have much opportunity to observe their pupils in situations other than the classroom. Furthermore, it is likely that many teachers judge pupils' interpersonal statuses entirely on the basis of overt behavior without realizing that such behavior is not always a true reflection of inner feelings. Others are too much influenced by some one trait which they observe in a child, such as generosity or bossiness, without realizing that pupils are attracted to one another, not on the basis of particular traits, whether good or bad, but on the basis of their total personalities.

It seems certain, then, that teachers need the kind of objective

---

8 N. L. Gage, G. S. Leavitt, and G. C. Stone, "Teachers' Understanding of Their Pupils and Pupils' Rating of Their Teachers," *Psychological Monographs,* No. 21 (Washington, D.C.: American Psychological Association, 1955).

9 N. E. Gronlund, "The Accuracy of Teachers' Judgments Concerning the Sociometric Status of Sixth-Grade Pupils," *Sociometry Monographs,* No. 25 (New York: Beacon House, Inc., 1951).

10 N. E. Gronlund, *Sociometry in the Classroom* (New York: Harper & Brothers, 1959), p. 166.

11 *Ibid.,* p. 166.

data obtained from sociometric and reputation measurements if they are to adequately evelute the social adjustments of their pupils.

Reliability and Validity

The two areas which are the topics of most inquiries about tests are the areas of reliability and validity. Briefly stated, the term *reliability* refers to the degree to which scores on a particular test can be shown to be constant for the same individuals over varying time intervals. Likewise, briefly stated, the term *validity* refers to the extent to which any testing instrument can be shown to measure what it purports to measure.

Reliability. In evaluating the results from sociometric testing it is important to note that what is considered under the topic of "reliability of measurement" is really the constancy or the stability of choice behavior. The question is: Do pupils respond to each other on similar choice-criteria very much the same on different occasions several weeks or several months apart? The first response to this question is that a very high degree of exact agreement over any considerable time interval is neither expected or desirable. This is true because it is well-known that interpersonal feelings are not static, and also because some changes in the direction of richer socialization is, from a sociometric point of view, considered desirable. However, it is also true that greater confidence can be placed in the results of sociometric testing if it can be shown that these results are fairly predictive of interpersonal affiliations over periods of several weeks or months or longer. Teachers are much more likely to take sociometric scores seriously if they have reason to believe that the pupils who are high will continue to have high choice-value and that those of average or low status will likewise retain, on the whole, their relative ranks, unless something unusual is done to aid particular individuals.

Space does not permit an adequate review of the evidence on the stability of choice behavior over varying time intervals, but it can be stated with confidence that the findings from approximately twenty investigations show a substantial constancy of choice-status in school groups over a period of several months, as evidenced by correlation coefficients falling between .56 and .76. Of course, much depends on the size of the group tested, the number of choices made by each pupil, and the kind of choice-criterion used. In general, the higher correlations are found when the classes consist of approximately thirty pupils, when five or more choices are made by each child, and when a fairly comprehensive criterion is utilized. Gronlund,[12] for example, found an average stability coefficient of .75 in nine upper elementary school classes over a four-month interval when choices were made for work companions. Likewise, in a series of studies Bonney[13] has reported stability coefficients ranging from .67 to .84 between total choices received by elementary school children from one grade level to the next when composite scores based on several sociometric tests throughout a year were used. These findings apply only to total choices received. There is less stability when individual-to-individual choosing is considered. In other words, although there is considerable flux in person-to-person interactions the overall group structure generally remains quite stable over periods of several months or longer. This is especially true among older children and adolescents.

Validity. Are sociometric measurements valid? This is a difficult question to answer because of the lack of any clear-cut standard of reference with which to verify the results of sociometric testing. This difficulty has led some writers in this field, such as Jennings,[14] to state that sociometric choices have "face validity" since they are direct measures of the phenomenon under investigation. In other words, if a fifth grader, John, says that he would like to sit near William, who is to deny the validity of this expressed desire, especially when it is noted that the test is not one of actual association but one of wish or aspiration. In spite of the strength of the "face validity" point of view, many writers in the sociometric field believe that in order to establish the functional value of sociometric data it is necessary to show that these data are related to, or are predictive of, other forms of evidence bearing on the personal-social adjustments of group members.

Reviewing briefly these forms of evidence, it can be shown, first (as previously indicated in this chapter), that teachers' judgments

---

[12] *Ibid.*, p. 125.

[13] M. E. Bonney, "The Relative Stability of Social, Intellectual and Academic Status in Grades II to IV and the Interrelationships Between These Various Forms of Growth," *Journal of Educational Psychology*, 34 (1943), pp. 88–102.

[14] H. H. Jennings, *Leadership and Isolation* (New York: Longmans, Green & Co., Inc., 1950), p. 27.

of pupils' socio-acceptance-positions correlate moderately with sociometric findings. Also a number of studies by Biehler,[15] Bonney,[16]
Byrd,[17] and others have shown considerable correspondence between the social behavior of children, as determined by systematic
adult observations and their sociometric test standings; this is particularly true when those who are high in choice-status are contrasted with those who are low.

If we assume that choices given in a sociometric test are valid
indicators of preferred interpersonal associations, then it should
follow that when these choices are made the basis for assignments
within a group there should be evidence of improved morale and
efficiency in this group. That this is the case in most populations
that have been tested for this purpose is revealed in a comprehensive
survey by Mouton, Blake, and Fruchter[18] of research conducted in
military, business, and educational organizations. Generally, socio-
metrically formed groups, as compared with those in which preferences are ignored, are characterized by more cooperative attitudes
and greater mutual support as well as by better records of performance.

Finally, if sociometric data accurately reflect interpersonal feelings, there should be some relationship between these data and
other ways of assessing personal-social adjustments. Numerous
studies (such as those by Bonney,[19] Kuhlen and Lee,[20] and Northway[21] have presented data on this topic using reputation measurements, personality self-ratings, problem check lists, and projective
tests. By way of a general summary of these investigations, it can
be stated that when total populations are considered, the over-all

---

[15] R. F. Biehler, "Companion Choice Behavior in the Kindergarten," *Child
Development,* 25 (1954), pp. 45–50.

[16] M. E. Bonney, "Social Behavior Differences Between Second Grade Children
of High and Low Sociometric Status," *Journal of Educational Research,* 48
(1955), pp. 481–95.

[17] E. Byrd, "A Study of Validity and Constancy of Choices in a Sociometric
Test," *Sociometry,* 14 (1951), pp. 175–81.

[18] J. S. Mouton, R. R. Blake, and B. Fruchter, "The Validity of Sociometric
Responses," *Sociometry,* 18 (1955), pp. 181–206.

[19] M. E. Bonney, "Personality Traits of Socially Successful and Socially Un-
successful Children," *Journal of Educational Psychology,* 34 (1943), pp. 449–72.

[20] R. G. Kuhlen and B. J. Lee, "Personality Characteristics and Social Acceptability in Adolescence," *Journal of Educational Psychology,* 34 (1943), pp.
321–40.

[21] M. L. Northway, "Outsiders: A Study of the Personality Patterns of
Children Least Acceptable to Their Age Mates," *Sociometry,* 7 (1944), pp. 10–25.

relationship between sociometric scores and scores obtained from these other types of assessments are frequently of only moderate magnitude or are definitely low. However, when those who are high in choice-status are contrasted with those who are low, the high ones in all studies possess some personality advantages over the low ones. This does not mean that all highly acceptable individuals are near-perfect examples of good personality. As a matter of fact, research shows that those high in sociometric status have some faults and weaknesses, and a few of them have serious personal problems. These findings emphasize that a person can have high preference value in the eyes of his peers and yet be struggling with various kinds of worries, anxieties, and sources of interpersonal frictions.

It may be concluded, then, that sociometric tests, in addition to revealing directly the interpersonal aspirations of the members of a group, are also significant indicators of a wide range of personal assets, especially those essential to making contributions to successful group functioning.

Measuring Changes
in Level of Socialization

A common weakness of many school programs which are designed to promote better socialization among children is that no objective measurements for evaluating the results are used. A teacher may be sure that he has greatly improved the interpersonal relationships among his pupils but he has no evidence to present to his supervisor or principal. With adequate use of sociometric data such evidence is available. What kinds of data are most appropriate for this purpose? These are given below and are stated in terms of the kind of data which would show an increase in level of socialization over a time interval.

Increase in positive choosing. When the amount of positive choosing between the members of a class increases over a time interval, an expansion of affiliative feelings among the pupils is indicated. This is measured simply by counting the total positive choices given by the class as a whole at the two different testing times. For this measurement to be possible, no arbitrary limit can be placed on the number of choices which each child can give on either testing. When the increase in volume of positive choosing is ten or fifteen per cent or more, this is certainly an indication of a better social climate for group living and for learning.

When the increase in positive choosing over a time interval is spread throughout a sociometric distribution, there would be some reduction in the number of isolates and rejectees. This obviously promotes social integration since the fewer the members of any class who feel "left out" entirely from social rewards, the fewer sore spots there will be in the social processes.

Increase in mutualities. A group will be more socially integrated when a high proportion of the feelings toward particular individuals are reciprocated, since this means more interpersonal satisfactions. One-way attachments, however, are not total losses because any positive feeling held toward others in a group helps create a more favorable social milieu. Increase or decrease in mutualities can be measured by counting the changes in the number of pupils who chose each other, especially those who chose each other as a first or second level preference.

Increase in positive choosing between those in the upper fourth of a sociometric distribution. The value of this kind of choosing is that it shows mutual support among the ones having the most social status. One of the most disintegrating conditions in any group is found when there are conflicting factions among those of high status, whether their status is based on ability, leadership, or social acceptance. When one half or more of those in the upper fourth choose each other on a sociometric criterion, evidence of mutual support and of unity among the leaders is indicated.

Increase in discriminative choosing. "Discriminative choosing" is that which is differentiated according to the nature of specific criteria, as opposed to choosing on the basis of personal attraction irrespective of particular competencies. This kind of evaluation is possible only when several different choice-criteria, varying in nature, are presented at both beginning and end testing, as for example: (1) Which children would you like to have as best friends? (2) Which ones would you like to be in a group with to prepare a one-act play? (3) Which ones would you prefer to have on your side in playground games?

Since these three criteria involve different kinds of traits and skills, there should be considerable difference in the choice-process in a class in which these three criteria are presented. In a group which becomes more socially mature over a period of time, such as one semester, there should be evidence of greater discriminative choosing according to the nature of each criterion.

Broadening of cliques. Since cliques are inevitable because of interpersonal preferences, the principal way whereby growth toward a more positive social climate can be evaluated, in so far as cliques are concerned, is to measure the extent to which these cohesive in-groups are expanded in their memberships and the extent to which there are at least a few individuals who are chosen over clique boundaries. It is particularly important that members of exclusive cliques, that is, those who choose only within their own in-group, be stimulated to develop acceptance of some individuals outside their cliques.

Increase in choosing between individuals in different sub-groupings. Certainly one of the most important ways of evaluating improvements in social integration or cohesiveness within a school group is to measure the extent to which there has been an increase in choosing between members of various subgroupings, such as between boys and girls, and between bus-transported students and town students. Increase in this kind of choosing means not only greater probability of pleasant associations between individuals in different subgroupings but also that more pupils are evaluating each other on the basis of individual merits rather than particular categories. This is evidence of greater personal and social maturity.

Using Sociometric Data in
Classroom Management and Pupil Guidance

In addition to using sociometric data as a means of evaluating changes in level of socialization over different time intervals, such data can also be utilized in classroom management and in individual pupil guidance.

Forming of classroom subgroups. The forming of subgroups within a class, a homeroom, or a club is probably the most frequent use made of sociometric test results, especially when a specific and functional criterion is the basis for choices. In arranging such groups, the principal aim is to provide each pupil with the most favorable situation for his maximum development. This means that those pupils who receive the fewest choices must be given first consideration in regard to being placed with those whom they chose. Children who reject each other should never be placed together. In the lower grades groups would be limited to three or four, whereas in the middle and upper grades four to six pupils can generally work together effectively. Although it is difficult to determine exactly the specific effects of sociometric grouping because of other factors always being in operation in a typical classroom setting, a number of studies by Atkinson,[22] Buck,[23] Dineen and Garry,[24] and Minnis,[25] have shown that when sociometric groupings are utilized, along with various socialization efforts, there have been definite social gains. Most of these gains consist of reduction of isolates, better integration of cliques, increase of mutualities, and some decrease in cleavage among pupils in varying social classes.

Aids in interpersonal assessments. Some problems of classroom management are closely related to accurate assessments of interpersonal relationships. Every experienced teacher can probably recall examples of particular pupils who were overblamed, in the sense that no matter what happened they were suspected or definitely accused, often without justification. These overblamed children are nearly always isolates or group rejects. If a teacher is aware of this fact, he can appraise more objectively the reported misconduct of particular pupils. Also, with sociometric data a teacher can more accurately appraise class reactions to the few pupils who stand very high in social acceptability, since these pupils are generally credited with more skill and desirable qualities than they actually possess.

Another way in which sociometric testing can aid in school management is by locating trouble spots in interpersonal relationships. Especially when negative choices are required, it is possible to locate those clubs, homerooms, and regular classes in which a high degree of hostility exists between certain cliques or between other kinds of subgroupings. When such conditions are found, preventive action can be taken before some kind of overt social explosion occurs.

[22] G. Atkinson, "The Sociogram as an Instrument in Social Studies; Teaching and Evaluation," *Elementary School Journal,* 50 (1949), pp. 74–85.

[23] J. V. Buck, "The Sociometric Technique and the Teaching of General Science," *School Science and Mathematics,* 52 (1952), pp. 456–61.

[24] M. A. Dineen and R. Garry, "Effect of Sociometric Seating on Classroom Cleavage," *Elementary School Journal,* 56 (1956), pp. 358–62.

[25] N. I. Minnis, "Sociometry as a Guidance Technique," *National Elementary Principal,* 34 (1954), pp. 180–83.

Furthermore, even if no overt hostilities take place, such groups are unproductive and generate much personal unhappiness. Although there is no one course of action which will always bring desirable results, one of the most promising for dealing with intragroup antagonisms is to utilize sociometric choices for picking out the accepted leaders of a group and working through these pupils to initiate some attitude changes. It is particularly important to utilize these high-status individuals to help start some activities that will bring divergent elements together in pursuit of a common goal.

Aids in guidance work. Another use for sociometric data is in guidance work with individuals. In many instances the personal-social problems of a pupil can be much better understood when his acceptance-status in his classroom is known. Furthermore these data can frequently offer leads for improvement by showing which other pupils a particular problem child would like to relate to, and which ones, if any, would like to associate more closely with him. Also, follow-up studies of six and seven years by Kuhlen and Collister[26] and by Gronlund and Holmlund[27] have shown that sociometric data can be very useful in locating those pupils who are, on the one hand, most likely to drop out of school between the sixth and twelfth grades, and, on the other hand, who are most likely to become leaders in high school. These findings imply, first, that if students of good ability who are likely to drop out of school could be helped with their interpersonal relationships many of them would probably stay in school; and, second, that if the most likely leaders in high school can be located in the sixth grade every effort can be made to see that they don't drop out of school and that they are helped to attain maximum personality maturity.

---

[26] R. G. Kuhlen and E. G. Collister, "Sociometric Status of Sixth- and Ninth-Graders Who Fail to Finish High School," *Educational and Psychological Measurement,* 12 (1952), pp. 632–37.

[27] N. E. Gronlund and W. S. Holmlund, "The Value of Elementary School Sociometric Status Scores for Predicting Pupils' Adjustment in High School," *Educational Administration and Supervision,* 44 (1958), pp. 255–60.

CHAPTER VI

Personality Ratings

The rating is one of the oldest forms of personality assessment. In numerous business and military organizations ratings are frequently used as a basis for evaluation and promotion. Likewise, in most schools some form of personality evaluation through rating is utilized. These kinds of assessments are described and critically examined in this chapter.

Probably the most frequently used means of personality assessment in schools is self-rating. When this procedure is followed, the pupils are presented with a printed or mimeographed form containing a list of questions bearing on many aspects of personal and social adjustments. The major purpose of such testing is to discover how pupils evaluate themselves and also how they see themselves in relation to significant aspects in their environment, such as their parents, peer associates, and school requirements. The approach is quite direct and highly structured, as contrasted with the projective methods discussed in a preceding chapter. Although personality questionnaires are widely used, they have been subjected to some of the severest criticisms of all personality measurements, partly because of the structured nature of the instruments and the rigid scoring system used. Unlike projective-type tests the subject is not free to make responses which seem most appropriate to him or which reveal something unique about himself; instead, he must answer specific questions only, and these questions are scored quantitatively according to a predetermined key.

While these characteristics are the source of much criticism, they are also the basis for the chief claims to merit by the makers of self-rating questionnaires. These claims are based on the fact that the items and the scoring have been determined by approved statistical procedures, and the standardized answers make possible the construction of group norms.

Before considering further the merits and criticisms of these kinds of personality assessments, it will be well to examine some representative samples in this area of testing.

Some Typical Self-Rating Questionnaires

Typical of other self-rating personality questionnaires are the California Test of Personality and the Mental Health Analysis.[1] Both of these consist of a series of forms for different age levels, from those in elementary schools to adults. The test items for both these series consist of direct questions which are to be answered *yes* or *no;* thus, a highly structured type of response is demanded. Furthermore, a large proportion of the items in these two test series are transparent in the sense that their implications for one's personal adjustment are quite obvious, for example:

> Do you feel that no one at home loves you?
> Are most of the children smarter than you?
> Are you often worried about dangers that you cannot foresee?
> Have you often felt that you were left out of things you would like to do?

For the upper elementary school grades and the junior high school, a useful self-descriptive instrument is available in the Junior Inventory-Form S.[2] This inventory provides scores in five areas, namely: About Me and My School, About Me and My Home, About Myself, Getting Along with Other People, and Things in General. The pupils respond to each of the 168 statements by checking it as a *big problem, a middle-sized problem, a little problem,* or *no problem.* Then they review all their answers and encircle the three problems which they would most like to have solved. Norms are based on 3000 cases which were selected through a process of stratified sampling. Some sample questions are:

> I wish teachers would tell me when I've done a good job.
> I wish my parents liked my friends better.
> I need to learn to stick up for my rights.
> I want to learn how to dance.

The authors of the Junior Inventory point out in their manual that the results of this self-descriptive scale can be used as an aid in

---

[1] Both published by the California Test Bureau, Del Monte Research Park, Monterey, California.

[2] Published by Science Research Associates, 57 W. Grand Ave., Chicago 10, Illinois, 1954.

curriculum planning, in selecting topics for discussion at parent-teacher meetings, in sensitizing teachers to pupils' problems, and in counseling with individuals.

Another instrument which could very well be used in conjunction with the Junior Inventory is titled What I like to Do—An Inventory of Children's Interests.[3] This inventory yields a profile of degrees of interest in the following areas: Art, Music, Social Studies, Active Play, Quiet Play, Manual Arts, Home Arts, and Science. The results obtained with this scale could offer leads in meeting some of the problems indicated on the Junior Inventory.

A recently published instrument for obtaining self-ratings is given in the appendix of *Early Identification of Emotionally Handicapped Children in School.*[4] It has separate forms for boys and girls called "Thinking About Yourself." It is constructed to measure not only how each child views himself but also how he would like to be. This method is illustrated by the following item:

This boy likes to do
daring things.

Always   Frequently   Seldom   Never

Are you like him?

Do you want to be
like him?

The extent to which a pupil checks the same columns for both questions indicates how well he is satisfied with himself as he is now; the greater the differences in the columns checked, the greater is a child's discrepancy score. Neither a high degree of satisfaction nor a high degree of dissatisfaction is considered most desirable from a mental health standpoint. There are fifty-three items for boys and girls in each form.

Two additional scales which are designed to measure the self-concepts of upper-elementary grade pupils, together with differences between actual and ideal self-concepts, are given in two journal articles.[5]

---

[3] Published by Science Research Associates, 57 W. Grand Ave., Chicago 10, Illinois.

[4] Eli M. Bower, "Early Identification of Emotionally Handicapped Children in School," *American Lectures in Psychology,* No. 404 (Springfield, Ill.: Charles C. Thomas, Publisher, 1960).

[5] H. V. Perkins, "Changing Perceptions of Self," *Childhood Education,* 34 (1957), pp. 82–84; and L. P. Lipsett, "A Self-Concept Scale for Children," *Child Development,* 29 (1958), pp. 463–72.

A self-rating personality questionnaire, typical of many others, which can be used on the senior high school level, is the California Inventory by Gough.[6] Norms, based on samplings in twenty states, are given for boys and girls separately and also for a number of adult groups. This inventory consists of 480 direct questions which are to be answered either True or False. From the several examples given below it will be evident that most of the items in this scale are transparent, in that each respondent can sense immediately whether a True or False answer would be considered desirable or undesirable. The examples are:

> It is pretty easy for people to win arguments against me.
> I daydream very little.
> The future seems hopeless to me.
> I have a natural talent for influencing people.

Even though a testee is aware of the favorable or unfavorable implications of an item, however, it does not necessarily follow that this awareness affects his answer; furthermore, he does not know how any particular answer will be scored for various traits.

Teachers and other school personnel who are concerned with personality evaluation in the elementary school will find an excellent discussion of problems, theories, and methods bearing on self-rating instruments in *Anxiety in Elementary School Children*.[7] This book describes the steps in the development and validation of two scales for measuring anxiety—one dealing with test anxiety and the other with more general aspects of anxiety among children of school age. Both these scales are based on intensive research and critical analysis and should be examined by anyone interested in evaluating personality variables through self-ratings.

Among the more recently developed personality self-rating instruments which are suitable for high school students are those produced by Cattell.[8] These inventories are labeled IPAT Self-Analysis Form, IPAT Contact Personality Factor Test, and IPAT High School Personality Questionnaire. All of these instruments are the product of

---

[6] Published by the Consulting Psychologists Press, Inc., Palo Alto, California, 1956.

[7] Sarason, *et al., Anxiety in Elementary School Children* (New York: John Wiley & Sons, Inc., 1960).

[8] Published by the Institute for Personality and Ability Testing, 1602 Coronado Drive, Champaign, Illinois.

many years of intensive factor-analysis research. This fact encourages confidence that the measured traits are consistent entities in a wide range of people and are relatively independent variables.

An inventory designed for high school students and adults is the Kuder Preference Record-Personal-Form.[9] This instrument concentrates on the measurement of those personal qualities which are considered essential in various types of occupations. Separate norms are given for males and females.

Teachers and counselors who wish to become acquainted with all the more reputable devices for measuring personality, together with critical evaluations of them, will find this material readily available in the *Fifth Mental Measurements Yearbook*.[10]

Criticism and Evaluation

For many years self-rating questionnaires have been extensively evaluated both from the standpoint of personality theory and that of accumulated evidence. This evaluation is still going on and apparently will be continued for quite some time. The kind of assessment made by a particular writer seems to depend partly upon the evidence and partly upon his psychological frame of reference which leads him to favorable or unfavorable conclusions regarding that evidence. Representative of the more recent books which present a critical and yet, on the whole, a favorable evaluation of personality questionnaires is that by J. P. Guilford;[11] representative of those which present not only a critical but also a highly unfavorable assessment is *Measurement for Guidance*.[12]

It can be stated that, on the whole, personality self-ratings are fairly reliable, since nearly all coefficients of reliability for total scores for the better established inventories fall between .72 and .86, with a few reporting figures as high as .88 and .91 for particular groups. Although the lower coefficients mentioned above are not high enough to warrant strong confidence in the stability of individ-

---

[9] Published by Science Research Associates, 57 W. Grand Ave., Chicago, Illinois, 1952.

[10] Oscar K. Buros, ed., *Fifth Mental Measurements Yearbook* (Highland Park, N.J.: Gryphon Press, 1959).

[11] J. P. Guilford, *Personality,* Chap. 8 (New York: McGraw-Hill Book Co., Inc., 1959).

[12] J. W. Rothney, P. J. Danielson, and R. A. Heimann, *Measurement for Guidance,* Chap. 8 (New York: Harper & Brothers, 1959).

ual scores (and especially of separate trait scores), it seems from our present evidence that most subjects do not vary greatly in the kind of over-all picture they present of themselves on personality inventories from one testing to another over short time intervals.

By far the most serious problems concerning the construction of personality inventories have centered around the question of validity. Do these instruments actually measure what they purport to measure? If a pupil answers the questions in such a manner that he comes out with a high rating for "ascendency," is he really outstanding in this trait; likewise, if his answers rank him very low in "confidence," is he really seriously lacking in this trait? The major problem in validity is to set up criteria of what is "really true" and then to relate the questionnaire scores to these criteria. These criteria have generally consisted of:

1. Ratings by close associates such as fellow students or co-workers, or by immediate supervisors such as teachers or foreman.

2. Records of performance in particular areas in which certain traits are presumably involved, such as success in selling or in various kinds of leadership roles.

3. Degrees of differences between questionnaire scores of groups having known characteristics, such as neuro-psychiatric patients as contrasted with normal individuals, leaders in school vs. nonleaders, or delinquents vs. nondelinquents.

In summary, the manuals for nearly all the better-known inventories present some data bearing on these three types of validity and, quite generally, the relationships reported are not high; some are of moderate size (correlations in the .40's and .50's), and some are definitely low. This means that the evidence for the external validity of personality questionnaires leaves much to be desired. Probably the most convincing evidence has been accumulated under the third validity criterion stated above, since nearly all reports show differences in the expected directions. These differences, however, are not usually statistically reliable except when rather extreme groupings are contrasted.

In addition to external criteria of validity, all makers of personality self-rating instruments present data on validity by internal consistency. This procedure involves the selection of items which correlate positively with the total scores or with certain trait-syndromes.

When this is done, there can be greater confidence that particular traits or personality patterns are being measured since the items retained show a tendency to hang together and to discriminate in the same direction when the inventory is administered to varying populations. The most statistically refined method which is used in this procedure is factor analysis. Although most of the currently used personality self-rating scales can show fairly satisfactory internal consistency, this kind of evidence can only supplement, but not substitute for, the kinds of external criteria described above.

In conclusion, the point must be emphasized that the validity of self-rating questionnaires is unsatisfactory, especially in working with individuals. This conclusion should be kept in mind by teachers and counselors. They should regard self-ratings not necessarily as factual data but as possible sources of leads in understanding pupils or as a basis for conferences. That these are the kinds of uses made of self-rating instruments in some schools is indicated from a survey of 510 secondary schools in California.[13] In responding to a questionnaire a very large majority of the principals of these schools stated that the chief uses made of personality self-ratings were in "identifying students with possible problems" and as "guides for use in interviews with students."

Criticisms of Personality Self-Ratings

Teachers and counselors who use self-rating instruments should be well aware of the more frequent criticisms of this form of personality assessment. These are: (1) the question of honesty of responses, (2) lack of self-knowledge, and (3) atomistic scoring.

Honesty of responses. A special aspect of the validity of personality questionnaires concerns the honesty of answers. Do the respondents to these instruments answer according to their beliefs or do they falsify their answers in an effort to make a good impression, to gain some advantage for themselves, to uphold their pride, or possibly to express their hostility toward the examiner or the test situation? These questions have never been answered to the complete satisfaction of the critics of questionnaires, although many

---

[13] Carl A. Larson and William H. McCreary, "Testing Programs and Practices in California Public Secondary Schools," *California Journal of Secondary Education,* Vol. XXXI, No. 7 (November 1956).

studies, such as those reviewed by Guilford,[14] have been conducted on these points.

One practical suggestion emanating from the discussions of possible falsifications of answers is for schools to administer personality questionnaires under conditions which assure the pupils that their scores will in no way be used against them. This is done, in a broad sense, by building up mutual trust between pupils and school staff members (especially teachers) in regard to all their relationships, and in a more specific sense, by telling the pupils at the time of the questionnaire administration that their answers will be confidential and will be used only to help in understanding their needs. Under conditions of mutual trust there is no more reason to assume that pupils will generally falsify their answers to a personality questionnaire than to assume that they will falsify their responses in other areas of association with people. Some evidence on this point is indicated by the fact that in any administration of a self-rating instrument, under the conditions mentioned above, a good many pupils will mark themselves low on many items. A few will almost always rate themselves low on practically all traits measured. These comments are not meant to imply that falsification should not be a matter of concern in interpreting self-ratings, but rather that this problem is not serious enough to invalidate their use.

Lack of self-knowledge. The second criticism of self-rating questionnaires is that, even though the testees do not falsify their answers, most of them do not know themselves well enough to give accurate answers. This criticism is based on the assumption that a good many people are not only limited in self-reflection and insight but are also characterized by unconsciously motivated self-defense mechanisms which prevent accurate appraisal of their own behavior. This certainly is a valid criticism, but the degree to which it can be applied to any one individual is very difficult to determine since we have no generally accepted criterion of what his traits are in fact.

In answer to this criticism Guilford[15] points out that a large proportion of the items in the better constructed inventories do not necessitate self-insight; rather they require only a report on observable facts or on fairly obvious overt behavior, as illustrated in such items as:

---

14 J. P. Guilford, *op. cit.*
15 *Ibid.*, pp. 191–92.

Have you ever kept a personal diary?
Do you prefer to work alone rather than with others?
I very much like hunting.
I like to talk before groups of people.
I have never done anything dangerous for the thrill of it.

Guilford further remarks that a personality inventory better serves its purpose if the psychological import of a large number of the items are not evident to the testee. He says that the purpose is to score him on traits that he does not know about by asking him questions that pertain to common things that he does know about. Undoubtedly, much more attention needs to be given, in the construction of personality questionnaires, to the selection of items which can be shown to be within the experience level and the intellectual comprehension of the great majority of pupils of any given age.

Atomistic scoring. The third major criticism of personality questionnaires concentrates on the atomistic procedure for arriving at total scores on an entire inventory as well as on part scores on particular traits. Reference is made to the practice of adding up responses to a wide range of items—all of which are considered to be measuring a certain designated trait. Questions can well be asked as to whether any trait, not to mention one's whole personality, can be adequately described by adding together the quantitatively scored responses to a list of specific questions. Does this not ignore the quality of wholeness, of unity, and of dynamic interaction of parts? This would certainly seem to be true. The critics point out that it is not just the number of items listed under a particular trait which a person checks as True or False that is most significant in understanding his personality, but rather the extent to which certain items are charged with emotional content or are viewed either with much enthusiasm or with great concern.

This weakness of limitation in scoring procedure should warn teachers and counselors against regarding a personality self-rating as a "picture" of a pupil's personality. What is chiefly lacking is an over-all, functional, integrated picture of the total person. Furthermore, the quantitative scoring and the precise graphs which can be drawn from the data may cause teachers to look upon each child's so-called personality picture as being so stable and final that nothing can be done to help him change unfavorable traits or to reach even more mature levels in areas in which he is shown to be strong.

In conclusion, it can be stated that although self-rating inventories are subject to serious criticisms, they can be used through group testing to screen out those pupils who probably need extra help in personal adjustments. Furthermore, these ratings are often fruitful sources for the study of particular individuals in reference to how they view themselves or how they are willing to present themselves to their adult supervisors. These instruments should never be regarded as personality *tests,* and they should never be used as a sole basis for personality assessment but always in conjunction with other kinds of information about each pupil.

Teacher Ratings of Pupils' Personality Traits

Teachers frequently make evaluative statements about pupils' personality traits in such remarks as: "Mary is too dominating," "Joan is too bossy," "Henry is such an agreeable child," or "Jack is bright but he is lazy."

What is gained by obtaining such evaluations on a rating scale instead of by occasional verbal statements? The answer is that the rating scale method is much more comprehensive in the number of traits on whch evaluations are made; ratings are obtained on all pupils in a class rather than on just a few who are outstanding, and the ratings can be quantified so that one child can be more readily compared with another; also ratings on the same child can be compared by different raters and over varying time intervals.

Obviously, personality trait ratings of one person by another have limitations and should never be considered by themselves to be adequate descriptions of another's personality. Such ratings are known to be heavily influenced by subjective and unconscious factors within the rater. In other words, although ratings are presumably based on objective observations of another person's behavior, it is well-known that these assessments are very much affected by one's personal frame of reference, values, and unconscious motivations. A teacher, for example, who has repressed his own need for aggressiveness may rate an unusually active and self-assertive child as being difficult to manage, uncooperative, anti-social, or as showing delinquency trends. Another teacher who is himself self-assured and normally aggressive could very easily rate this same child as showing enthusiasm, alertness, spontaneity, and leadership qualities. Likewise, one teacher could view a highly docile child as being sweet, nice, lovable, and adorable; whereas another teacher with more perception into personality dynamics could very easily view this same child as being repressed, guilt ridden, suffering from inferiority feelings, and unhappy.

These examples illustrate how "halo effect" or "halo error" enters into ratings. When a rater has a generally favorable impression of an individual, this halo effect is very likely to cause him to overrate this person on most desirable traits; likewise, when a rater has a generally unfavorable impression of an individual he is very likely to underrate him on desirable traits and to overrate him on negative ones. This kind of error illustrates a more general point about ratings, namely, that most ratings of particular traits are based more on over-all assessments of the total person than upon detailed analysis of a specific behavior trend.

The tendency of teachers to be influenced in their judgments of pupils by the halo error is illustrated in a study by Lewis,[16] in which he revealed a consistent tendency among teachers in 453 schools to rate pupils as having desirable or undesirable personality traits very much in accordance with their previous classification of these pupils as falling into one of the following categories: normal, mentally retarded, genius, or a distinct problem. While it is no doubt true that such groupings of pupils are also accompanied by personality differences, other evidence shows that these differences in respect to desirable and undesirable traits are not so distinct.

Homemade rating scales. Many large school systems produce their own rating scales, usually through the division of research with the aid of supervisors and teachers. Such scales are not standardized and may be lacking in statistical refinements, but they may be more adapted to local needs. Furthermore, when supervisors and teachers participate in developing a rating scale they are more ego-involved in it and consequently more likely to make conscientious use of it.

---

[16] W. D. Lewis, "Some Characteristics of Children Designated as Mentally Retarded, as Problems, and as Geniuses by Teachers," *The Journal of Genetic Psychology,* 70 (1947), pp. 29–51.

When a school system undertakes the production of a "home-made" rating scale, the persons assigned to this particular responsibility are faced with the question of which traits to include. This may be answered by asking a large number of teachers and supervisors to submit lists of traits which they consider most essential for understanding pupils.

It would be desirable to have, however, a more objectively determined basis for selecting the traits to be included. Psychologists have not agreed on a list of basic personality traits, which, presumably, should be the source for selecting items for a personality rating scale. Such a list may not be feasible since traits are not static entities, but rather dynamic processes, which, though they are characterized by considerable consistency within any one individual, nevertheless vary greatly in their functional significance within different total personalities. Probably Cattell,[17] using factor analysis methods, has done the most work in this country in trying to select a list of basic personality traits. He has developed a list of forty-two variables, indicated through many years of research with large group testing and statistical analysis. Members of a school staff who would like to prepare a rating scale would do well to consult this source for items to include.

Published scales. One pupil rating scale which has been around a long time but which still appears to be useful is the Haggerty-Olson-Wickman Behavior Rating Schedules.[18] On Schedule A of these forms the teacher is asked to check each pupil in reference to the frequency with which he has engaged in each of fifteen behavior problems, such as cheating, bullying, and imaginative lying. On Schedule B a teacher is asked to rate each child on thirty-five traits, each of which is described on a continuum, as illustrated below in reference to the trait of courage:

Does he lack nerve, or is he courageous?

White-livered, fearful	Gets "cold feet"	Will take reasonable chances	Resolute	Dare-devil
(4)	(3)	(1)	(2)	(5)

---

[17] R. B. Cattell, *Personality and Motivation-Structure and Measurement* (New York: Harcourt, Brace & World, 1957), pp. 813–17.
[18] Published by Harcourt, Brace & World, New York: 1930.

Although this kind of rating scale represents one of the better forms for obtaining valid ratings, it is subject to the halo error discussed above. One way to reduce this kind of error is to avoid having each pupil rated on all traits at one time. Probably the best method is not to have all the traits listed continuously on one form but to have only one trait on a page, together with all the individuals to be rated. This procedure forces the rater to react to each ratee on each trait separately and, presumably, helps to break up the tendency to rate many individuals high or low on all traits because of positive or negative over-all judgments. Guilford presents a form for this kind of rating in his discussion of graphic rating scales.[19]

Another type of published rating scale is available in an instrument designated Behavior Description Chart, developed under the direction of Havighurst.[20] Each of the eighteen trait variables included in the Behavior Description Chart is described by five items, as illustrated in the following sample:

A. Makes sensible, practical plans.
B. Breaks rules.
C. Needs much prodding.
D. Dislikes criticism.
E. Accepts responsibility when it is assigned to him.

The rater is instructed to check the one item which a particular ratee is *most like* and the one which he is *least like*. This is called the forced-choice technique since the rater is forced by the instructions to check characteristics at opposite extremes within each trait variable. The theory behind this technique is that it will help reduce the tendency of most raters to be overly generous and lenient in favorable ratings of others. Although it has no doubt succeeded in this objective to some extent, a number of students of personality testing, such as Guilford[21] and Vernon,[22] have pointed out that the forced choice technique has not succeeded in this purpose as well as was first expected. Furthermore, many raters find it irritating to have to check two opposite kinds of items in each grouping since they feel

[19] Guilford, *op. cit.*, p. 143.

[20] In *Studying Children* and *Training Counselors in a Community Program*, ed. Robert J. Havighurst, "The Youth Development Series," No. 2 (Chicago: University of Chicago Press, 1953).

[21] Guilford, *op. cit.*, p. 145.

[22] P. E. Vernon, *Personality Tests and Assessments* (New York: Holt, Rinehart & Winston, Inc., 1953), p. 113.

that in some instances they are forced to make arbitrary and unfair ratings.

Teachers and guidance personnel, however, will find the Behavior Description Chart an interesting device to use. It has been shown by Havighurst and his associates to be very useful in selecting pupils who are regarded by teachers as being outstanding in leadership or in aggressive and withdrawal types of maladjustment.

Suggestions for Improving Ratings

Numerous studies have shown that most people can be helped to improve the validity of their ratings as a consequence of special training. Such training is accomplished through prepared speeches, group discussions, selected reading materials, and individual conferences. The principal aim of such efforts, when conducted in school situations, is to help teachers become more fair, accurate, and objective in their perceptions of pupils' behavior characteristics. These goals are accomplished primarily by:

1. Helping teachers avoid, or at least reduce, the "halo effect."
2. Helping teachers to be less influenced by common stereotypes in regard to students who belong to particular races, ethnic groups, or social classes.
3. Helping teachers realize that some of their personality adjustments, through the process of projection, are important factors in determining what they see in others.

Obviously, all three of these goals are difficult to reach. Indeed, one would be naive to suppose that great progress could be made with most teachers on these objectives; however, as already stated, adequate training efforts can make a difference. Such a training program is more likely to be successful when continuous efforts are made by administrators to involve teachers personally in pupil evaluations, when a competent resource person is available for aid in conducting the kind of training program required, and when some constructive use is actually made of the teacher ratings.

Administrative practices also have a bearing on the validity of teachers' ratings of pupils. If a supervisor or a principal uses teachers' ratings in any way as a threat to their feelings of competence or to their status in the school system, it would be expected that the validity of their ratings would be greatly reduced. This kind of threat can be posed when an administrative official implies that if a teacher gives his pupils many low ratings, it is an indication that he has failed to live up to all his obligations as a teacher. Also, a threat can be posed if an administrative official lets a teacher know that his ratings are considered to be erroneous or invalid since they do not agree with ratings given by other teachers. The principal effect of such a statement, when it circulates throughout a school staff, is to induce a large percentage of the teachers to collaborate on their ratings and thus render all of them less valid. Although a certain teacher's ratings may be inconsistent with the others, they must nevertheless be taken as a valid portrayal of this person's impressions of particular pupils. All ratings should be shown in profile form; they should not be averaged because an average rating hides significant differences between raters and may not accurately represent any one rating.

All experienced school administrators have probably discovered that some teachers' judgments of pupils are much more in accord with objective records about these pupils than are those of other teachers. Numerous studies have been conducted to find what factors, if any, are reliably associated with the ability to make accurate judgments of the personality traits of one's associates. These studies have included data on sex differences, intelligence, family size, college major, social class level, and a wide range of personality characteristics.[23]

All this research has, for the most part, resulted in inconclusive findings. It does seem fairly certain, though, that good judges of others, as compared with poor judges, are likely to be more intelligent, to possess greater capacity for detached observations, and to be characterized by less egocentrism and greater self-insight. A school administrator who wishes to make maximum use of teachers' judgments of pupils' behavior would do well to follow all leads available in trying to determine which teachers on his staff make the most valid ratings.

---

[23] Guilford, *op. cit.,* pp. 150–52.

CHAPTER VII

Evaluation of Class Attitudes

The great majority of measurements taken in classrooms are obtained to assess the strengths and weaknesses of individuals. This is true of all standardized achievement testing, of intelligence testing, and of nearly all personality measurements. It is less true of sociometric testing since some over-all group characteristics can be obtained from these kinds of data.

In recent years a wide range of investigations have been concerned with assessments of groups as units. The focus of interest of these endeavors has been on such intangible factors as morale, climate of opinion, group attitudes, rapport, and group atmosphere. The methods and implications of these kinds of studies are of great importance to schools since teachers and administrative staff members are faced constantly with group situations. The quality of these groups, *as groups,* has a significant bearing on all types of learning and behavior adjustments within the school setting.

This statement obviously implies that there are influences at work within a group which are the result of interactions between the members and that these influences cannot be understood simply by knowing the individuals apart from the group situation. These interactions do not result in a mysterious "group mind," but they do result in ideas, attitudes, and feeling responses within the members —responses which are created by the group interaction processes and which would not exist in the same form and intensity if these same individuals were not allowed to interact. These psychological and social group processes are created as the members interact with each other in reference to group tasks, to the behavior of the group leader, and to how they regard each other on a purely personal basis. These three major kinds of interactions are constantly in operation in all school groups and they constitute what is variously called group morale, atmosphere, or climate.

A sensitive teacher is able to evaluate the morale of his class by noting particular kinds of behaviors which are indicative of good or poor attitudes toward the group situation. He can note, for example, the extent to which leadership roles in the class are invested with prestige, the degree of interest shown in discussing matters requiring group action, the amount of eager participation in group-sponsored activities, and the willingness of the class members to integrate their individual interests into a cooperative endeavor toward a group goal.

Use of Teacher-Pupil Interaction Analysis

In addition to observation of pupils' behavior, it is also possible to reach an assessment of the social climate of a class through teacher-pupil interaction analysis. This involves a procedure for systematically recording teacher-pupil contacts during regular class periods. This recording is done by one or two observers who sit in the back of the room. Usually, the major concentration is on the verbal responses of the teacher. These are the easiest to record on a prepared observation form and, furthermore, have proven to be valuable indexes to the social-emotional climate of school classes.

The first studies of this nature were conducted by Anderson and his associates.[1] Utilizing carefully obtained records of teachers' contacts with pupils, as well as pupils' contacts with each other, these investigators were able to show that the way a teacher treated pupils was heavily reflected in their behavior. In a classroom with a teacher whose contacts with children were largely of a dominating nature, there was much evidence of lassitude, easy distractability, and of either marked compliance with or marked rejection of the teacher. However, in a classroom with a more democratic teacher, who used what Anderson called "integrative contacts," there was much greater evidence of spontaneity, initiative, mutual aid between pupils, voluntary contributions, and constructive problem solving.

Since Anderson's pioneer work, other procedures, recording techniques, and methods of analysis for studying the social-

---

[1] Harold H. Anderson and Helen M. Brewer, "Studies of Teachers' Classroom Personalities, I: Dominative and Socially Integrative Behavior of Kindergarten Teachers," *Applied Psychology Monographs*, 6 (1945); and Harold H. Anderson and Joseph E. Brewer, "Studies of Teachers' Classroom Personalities, II: Effects of Teachers' Dominative and Integrative Contacts on Children's Classroom Behavior," *Applied Psychology Monographs*, 8 (1946).

emotional climate of classes have been developed by Bales,[2] Thelen,[3] and Withall.[4]

Flanders has reported on some intensive work at the University of Minnesota in analyzing the effects of different kinds of teacher-pupil interactions.[5] He and his associates have arrived at twelve categories for recording teacher-pupil-verbal-response behavior in the classroom. With the use of this recording procedure it is possible to assess the degree to which a teacher is meeting the social-emotional, as well as the intellectual, needs of the pupils.

Use of Prepared Instruments

In addition to informal observations and the use of interaction analysis in studying classroom morale and social climate, there are also available a number of more formally prepared instruments which can be used in diagnosing attitudes relating to various aspects of group functioning. These consist of questionnaires and rating scales and other more specialized devices.

Generalized attitude scales. Attitude scales of general usefulness have been developed under the direction of Remmers.[6] These scales are constructed so that a fairly wide range of topics may be utilized for measurement on any one scale. For example, A Scale to Measure Attitude Toward Any School Subject provides for five different subjects to be listed at the top of five columns. The students respond to the scale by putting a plus sign opposite each of the seventeen items on the scale that expresses their attitudes toward each of the subjects listed. It may be assumed that students' attitudes toward their school subjects are good indexes of group morale in these respective classes.

Other scales published by the Purdue University Center which

---

[2] Robert F. Bales, *Interaction Process Analysis* (Reading, Mass.: Addison-Wesley Publishing Company, Inc., 1950).

[3] H. A. Thelen, "Work Emotionality Theory of the Group as Organism," in *Psychology: A Study of a Science,* ed. Sigmund Koch (New York: McGraw-Hill Book Co., Inc., 1959), Vol. 3, pp. 544–611.

[4] J. Withall, "The Development of a Technique for the Measurement of Social-Emotional Climate in Classrooms," *Journal of Experimental Education,* 17 (1949), pp. 347–61.

[5] N. A. Flanders, "Teacher-Pupil Contacts and Mental Hygiene," *The Journal of Social Issues,* 15 (1959), pp. 30–39.

[6] H. H. Remmers, Division of Educational Reference, Purdue University Research Foundation, West Lafayette, Indiana.

could be used to measure various aspects of morale in school groups are: (1) A Scale for Measuring Individual and Group Morale, (2) A Scale for Measuring Attitudes Toward Any Defined Group, (3) High School Attitudes Scale. All the Purdue scales consist of seventeen items and are very easily administered and scored.

A group dimensions questionnaire. A comprehensive questionnaire for measuring thirteen aspects of group morale has been prepared by Hemphill.[7] This questionnaire consists of 150 items and is labeled Group Dimensions—the thirteen dimensions being: Autonomy, Control, Flexibility, Hedonic Tone, Homogeneity, Intimacy, Participation, Permeability, Polarization, Potency, Stability, Stratification, and Viscidity. Each respondent answers each question in reference to a particular group he is in by checking one of five alternatives. A profile is obtained on the basis of the composite answers of all the members of a group. By administering this questionnaire at two different times, it is possible to show what changes in group morale have been made as a result of particular socializing programs which may have been introduced. This instrument could not be used below the senior high school level and is most appropriate for voluntary groups, such as school clubs and church and community organizations, as contrasted with classes.

A projective instrument. Teachers who are interested in more specialized types of measurements will profit by examining a book by Libo entitled *Measuring Group Cohesiveness*.[8] This book presents data bearing on the development of a picture-projective-type test for measuring varying degrees of integration and isolation of individuals within social groups. Although a scoring or coding system is given, one of the most valuable uses of this instrument is found in studying the more qualitative aspects of the responses made by particular pupils as they describe what they think is happening in a series of drawings representing different group situations.

Experimental and unstandardized instruments. In some of our larger school systems a variety of experimental scales and techniques are being used to measure various aspects of class morale. One such

---

[7] J. K. Hemphill, "Group Dimensions—A Manual for Their Measurement" (Columbus, Ohio: Bureau of Business Research, Ohio State University).

[8] L. M. Libo, *Measuring Group Cohesiveness* (Ann Arbor, Mich: Research Center for Group Dynamics—Institute for Social Research of the University of Michigan, 1953).

instrument is The Draw-A-Teacher Technique which instructs the pupils to draw a teacher with a class.[9] These drawings are scored along three dimensions—Teacher Initiative, Psychological Distance, and Traditionalism in Classroom Organization. Interscorer agreement with this scale ranged from .84 to .93.

The Observation Schedule and Record[10] is a form which provides for recording specific events in a classroom and requires few inferences on the part of the observer. A total of fourteen dimensions have been developed for this scale but the four which bear most closely on classroom social climate are: Disorderly Pupil Behavior, Manifest Teacher Hostility, Pupil Leadership Activities, and Freedom of Movement. Interrater reliability in classifying events in these four categories ranged from .71 to .85.

My Class Inventory is another unstandardized measuring instrument.[11] It consists of forty-seven items concerning Halo, Disorder, and Climate. One of the major objectives in working with this instrument was to produce a questionnaire which would measure various aspects of pupil and teacher behavior apart from the "halo effect," that is, apart from the general feelings of like and dislike which pupils hold toward a teacher. This was accomplished by showing that the pupils' responses to eight items which clearly concerned personal feelings toward the teacher were significantly different from their responses to the groups of items concerning Disorder and Climate. Data for this analysis were obtained from forty-nine classes in the New York City public schools in grades three to six.

Some sample items from My Class Inventory are:

Are you proud to be in this class?	yes——no——
Do most of the pupils like the teacher?	yes——no——
Do the pupils often make so much noise that it is hard for you to work?	yes——no——
Are you always told what to do and when to do it?	yes——no——
Do the pupils ask a lot of questions?	yes——no——

---

[9] D. M. Medley and Alix A. Klein, "Studies of Teacher Behavior: Inferring Classroom Behavior from Pupil Responses," Division of Teacher Education, Board of Higher Education of the City of New York, 500 Park Avenue, New York 22, N.Y., 1956.

[10] Ibid.

[11] Ibid.

By using this inventory a teacher can obtain some very useful information in regard to how the class as a whole views him as well as how they view various aspects of class functioning. Furthermore, he can test the extent to which his perception of the classroom situation differs from that of the class by checking the items on the Class Inventory as he thinks the majority of the pupils will answer them and then comparing his answers with the class responses. In working with teachers who have used the inventory in this manner, the writers have found this kind of comparison to be a valuable source of stimulation for in-service training of teachers in developing greater understanding of group processes and teacher-pupil relationships.

In a study specifically designed to test the validity of the California F Scale (a measure of authoritarian attitudes), McGee developed several instruments for recording a teacher's classroom behavior in reference to the degree of teacher-pupil domination.[12] One of these, labeled Glossary: Classroom Behavior, is a very comprehensive list of teacher behavior and pupil responses, both verbal and nonverbal. The list is arranged with paired items, suitable for ratings. This scale should be examined by anyone interested in evaluating classroom social climate. In McGee's study the findings with the observational instruments were shown to correlate fairly well (.58) with authoritarian attitudes as these were measured by a revision of the California F Scale.

---

[12] Henry M. McGee, "Measurement of Authoritarianism and Its Relation to Teachers' Behavior," *Genetic Psychology Monographs,* 52 (1955), pp. 89–146.

CHAPTER VIII

The Case Study and
the Cumulative Record

The case study and the cumulative record, termed eclectic techniques in Chapter I, may be considered techniques only in the sense that they are special ways of organizing data collected by the use of numerous evaluative techniques.

The Case Study

A *formal* case study is a thorough investigation of all the information about a pupil which may be pertinent in solving some problem in his life. It is a written account which includes a pupil's life history as well as current data about his mental, physical, emotional, and social development or behavior. It is ordinarily utilized as a technique for solving only the more serious or complicated problem situations, and hence is limited in use to only a few pupils. The *informal* case study may or may not be put in writing, and it may include only a few data which are pertinent to a specific, rather isolated, or uncomplicated problem. This technique may be used in solving the adjustment problems of many pupils. For many years good teachers have used this technique consistently in their daily attempts to study the problems of individual children, to diagnose, and to apply treatment.

Advantages of the case study. "The case study is a primary tool of evaluation."[1] It has been a valuable tool to doctors and social workers for many years. Only relatively small numbers of teachers have used it, however, and the extent of use has most often been limited to rather thorough case studies of only exceedingly serious problem cases. Teachers in large numbers have not made use of case studies both because they have not known how to use them and because they have felt that the task was too time-consuming and too

---

[1] J. Wayne Wrightstone, Joseph Justman, and Irving Robbins, *Evaluation in Modern Education* (New York: American Book Company, 1956), p. 215.

complicated. Much of this fear of the case study has probably been due to a limited or narrow conception of it. Teachers conceive of it primarily as a formal or structured, detailed, and very thorough written account of a serious behavior problem case. Teachers would probably use the case study to a greater extent if they realized that the *informal* case study is not an awesome thing and that the values inherent in its use are basic and important as a fundamental part of an effective job of teaching.

The major advantages of the case study may be summarized as follows:

1. It takes a look at the "whole child." A good case study will examine all possible factors, mental, physical, social, and emotional, which may give some clue to the problem behavior.

2. Possibly one of the major advantages of the case study, for teachers, resides in the process or method which underlies successful use of it as a tool of evaluation. Inherent in the process, for successful use, is an understanding on the part of the teacher that there are reasons for children's behavior. Teachers can develop such an understanding if they will make use of case study techniques.

3. A case study can be reliable. This is particularly true in those cases which are handled by skilled workers who conclude their cases in a case conference, utilizing the insight of several co-workers to get more reliable interpretations.

4. It leads teachers to be more aware of the special problems of individual children, thereby helping to weaken the tendency to teach the same lesson to a whole class.

5. With increased use of the case study, teachers begin to see that, in reality, it is fundamentally a part of the teaching process itself.

6. Used with regularity as a part of the teaching process, teachers will find that they are discovering causes of behavior while problems are less serious, thereby reducing the number of serious problem situations which require formal and more extensive case studies.

7. As teachers observe and study the behavior of many pupils, it helps them to gain a better concept of normal behavior. This will help give them better perspective in interpreting negative and abnormal behavior when they encounter it.

8. In the process of studying one or a few children, teachers usually find that they become more aware of and sensitive to behavior symptoms in all the children.

9. The case study approach helps the school staff become aware of the pupil personnel services that are available both within the school

and within the community. It also develops an awareness of those aspects of the pupil personnel program which are nonexistent.

Relationship to other methods of evaluation. The case study uses data from all the evaluative techniques described in this book as well as data obtained from standardized and teacher-made tests. If comprehensive data from these varied techniques have been collected and recorded on the school's cumulative record forms (ordinary cumulative records usually are not complete enough where serious problems are involved), they will constitute the data needed for the case study. In turn, the completed case study is filed as an important part of the cumulative record folder.

Suggested parts of a formal case study.[2] The following outline for a case study is fairly typical of those you may see given by other authors. There is nothing sacred about this or any other outline. A good one needs to cover all the essential facets of a student's life history and be organized so that the parts may be readily seen for ease of comprehension and interpretation.

1. Statement of the reason for the case study. Some writers call this step "the statement of the problem." Others feel that the original reason for study may be discovered later to be only a symptom and, hence, prefer to term it the "reason" for the study.

2. Collection of data (much of which may already be found in the cumulative records).[3]
   a. Identifying data.
   b. Family history and home and neighborhood environment.
   c. Personality evaluation.
   d. Health history and present health status.
   e. Educational history and present status, including present mental age, achievement level, interests, aptitudes, social and emotional adjustment, and physical development.

3. Interpretation of the data, which should culminate in tentative hypotheses or a diagnosis of the causes underlying the problem behavior. In order to arrive at a more accurate diagnosis, it is considered good procedure to have several people involved in the case hold a conference.

---

[2] For an example of a case study written by an experienced teacher (her first attempt to do one), see Alfred Schwartz and Stuart C. Tiedeman, *Evaluating Student Progress in the Secondary School* (New York: Longmans, Green & Company, Inc., 1957), pp. 251–58.

[3] See Theodore L. Torgerson, *Studying Children* (New York: Holt, Rinehart & Winston, Inc., 1947), pp. 190–210, for detailed inventories which may be used as guides in collecting these data and for a case study form which may be used as a convenient method of organizing the data.

Such a "case conference" might include such people as the teacher or teachers, the principal, the parents, school psychologist, school or family doctor, social worker or visiting teacher, and perhaps others, depending on the nature or seriousness of the case.

4. Selection of therapy or remedial treatment which will most effectively alleviate the problem behavior.

5. Follow-up evaluation to investigate the effectiveness of the treatment. If treatment has not achieved results, review must be made of any one or all the preceding four steps.

Limitations of the case study. The following items constitute the chief limitations or weaknesses of the case study:

1. It is time-consuming.

2. It may be too subjective. The degree of subjectivity will depend upon the nature of the problem studied, the availability of objective data through the use of valid and reliable measuring instruments, and the qualifications or limitations of the person who does the case study.

3. Limitations of the teacher. The teacher may lack the necessary skills for collecting and interpreting data:

   a. He may not know what data are needed or the techniques to use in gathering them.

   b. He may not sufficiently understand the psychological principles of behavior and learning to make competent judgment in diagnosing and suggesting therapy in problem cases.

Cumulative Records

Cumulative records consist of all the data about an individual pupil which a school considers important enough to collect and record, usually in some organized way, for safekeeping from year to year. They are sometimes termed personnel records, permanent records, and accumulative records.

Prior to 1930, most schools were content to keep a record of only attendance and grades, kept in a book called the school register. There are still schools which have not advanced very far beyond this point. Many of the better schools over the country, however, have developed a rather complete and very adequate system of record-keeping. In these schools a wide variety of information is recorded: personal data, test scores, the results of many of the informal evaluation techniques described here, samples of pupils' work, notations about parent conferences, and so forth.

Place of cumulative records in evaluation. One unique aspect of cumulative records as a phase of evaluation is that they become the depository of all the evaluative data about an individual pupil which the teachers, counselors, and administrators in a school system think will be useful information for them. Teachers and counselors need all the information they can get which will give them clues to assess the mental, social, emotional, and physical adjustment problems of pupils—a comprehensive picture of the whole child. In addition, counselors at the secondary level need vocational interest and aptitude information to use in counseling students about vocational plans. Administrators are more interested in such things as attendance data and the results of the achievements testing program. Attendance data are used for state reports, which in many states determine the amount of state money for which a school is eligible. Achievement test results are used in reporting to the public on the effectiveness of school instruction. Complete and well-organized records, if put to use, will enable a school staff to attack and solve many of the adjustment problems of pupils.

Aside from being a depository for all the evaluative data which have been collected, cumulative records also give school people a longitudinal picture of the growth and development of each pupil. By noting trends over a period of years for any particular type of data, a more valid evaluation may be made than would be possible by looking at only a segment of the data.

Data usually collected. Only data which will be used should be collected as it is expensive in time, money, and filing space to collect unnecessary data. It is therefore recommended that school staffs cooperatively decide what they want to collect and record in the permanent cumulative record. Any suggested list of data to be collected should be checked by each local school system and adapted to its own needs.

Following is a list of items to include in a cumulative record system. It was drawn up by the National Committee on Cumulative Records after studying the results of a nationwide survey by the U.S. Office of Education of items included in cumulative record systems of the 1230 cities responding to the survey.[4]

---

[4] Federal Security Agency, U.S. Office of Education, *Handbook of Cumulative Records*, Bulletin No. 5 (Washington, D.C.: Government Printing Office, 1944), pp. 8–9.

Personal

    Name
    Date of birth
    Evidence of birth
    Place of birth
    Sex
    Color or race
    Residence of pupil and/or parents

Home and Community

    Names of parents or guardians
    Occupation of parents or guardians
    Are parents alive or deceased
    Ratings of home environment and/or economic status
    With whom does pupil live
    Birthplace of parents
    Language spoken in home
    Marital status
    Number of siblings, older and younger

Scholarship

    School marks by years and subject
    Special reports of failures
    Record of reading
    Rank in graduating class (with number in class)

Test Scores and Ratings

    General intelligence test scores
    Achievement test scores
    Other test scores
    Personality ratings

School Attendance

    Days present or absent each year
    Record of schools attended, with dates

Health

    (The following types of items are desirable if a school has a health program in which physicians and nurses are a part:)

    Complete health record, to be filled in by physician or nurse
    Record of physical disabilities
    Vaccination record
    Disease census

    (If a physician or nurse is not available for examining school children, a rating of the health of pupils may be made by the teachers, the type of rating depending upon the extent of the education of the teachers in health matters.)

Anecdotal Records

(If an anecdotal record system is to be used, a special form should be developed. Anecdotal records may be kept easily if filed in a folding type of cumulative record or filed where records are kept in envelopes.)

Miscellaneous

Employment record during school years
Vocational plans
Counselor's notes
Extracurricular activities
Follow-up record after leaving school (employment and further education)
Space for notations by teachers and others

An examination of this list will indicate that there is no mention made of the results of many of the informal evaluative techniques described in this book. These evaluations are not readily summarized to fit into a small space on a form. Most of them—checklists, case studies, samples of work, questionnaires, autobiographies, and so forth—are valuable for the details which they contain and would have to be filed as separate sheets inside the cumulative record folder.

Types of records. School systems having only a few items of information about individual pupils which they regularly record on permanent records use only a single card. Other schools keep a series of several single cards about different aspects of a child's growth which they file separately. Most of the schools which keep an adequate record of many aspects of pupils' growth have shifted to the use of a manila folder plus insert cards. They have forms printed on both the inside and outside pages. Frequently, this is not space enough to hold all the information collected, so they print 8½- by 11-inch card inserts for other information. In addition, the folder can be used as a file for anecdotal records, case studies, other informal evaluation data, notations about the results of parent-teacher conferences, and so forth.

Many school systems in the past have developed separate records for use with primary grades, intermediate grades, junior high and senior high school. Because of the problems of summarizing this information for transfer to the record-keeping system at the next higher level, schools in increasing numbers are developing record systems which include all the information needed for kindergarten through high school.

Uses. A complete system of cumulative records serves many purposes. It is useful for handling many continuing routine instructional and administrative matters and for helping to solve a variety of other problems as they arise. The following list of uses will help to indicate how versatile a good cumulative record system can be.

1. To save time in getting acquainted with new pupils so that plans may be made quickly to adjust the program of instruction to their needs. This would include the identification of exceptional children (slow and gifted) so that special programs could be planned for them.

2. To identify and help in properly diagnosing and treating all pupils who show evidence of behavior problems.

3. To help in locating scholastic strengths and weaknesses of pupils.

4. To be the source of information for conferences with parents.

5. To be the source of information for conferences with pupils. Many teachers and counselors use some of the records to encourage pupils to evaluate themselves.

6. To form the basic data needed for doing case studies. If the cumulative records are complete, most of the data for the case study will be readily available. It would then be possible for counselors or outside specialists or clinicians to study a case and arrive at suggestions for treatment very quickly.

7. To assist in determining pupils' grade placement, promotion, retention, acceleration, grouping within the classroom, or sectioning by ability.

8. To provide clues for possibly needed curriculum changes.

9. To provide important information to a new school when pupils transfer.

10. To provide information to counselors for talks with pupils about vocational or college plans.

11. To provide information to prospective employers or to college registrars.

12. To supply various branches of the military service with information which can be valuable to them in making better placement of personnel.

13. To provide administrators with the necessary data for state reports for accrediting purposes, state reports on eligibility for state funds, and so forth.

14. To provide administrators with data to use in relating to the public the achievements or shortcomings of the instructional program.

15. To serve as an evaluation instrument to study the effectiveness of the school program in the light of follow-up studies of graduates and drop-outs or of reports employers make of former pupils.

Characteristics of good cumulative records

1. Good cumulative records contain as complete information as possible about all aspects of all pupils' growth and development over the period of years they are in school. Newer record-keeping systems include a greater variety of test data and the results of informal evaluations of personal, social, and emotional adjustment. Older systems were limited, for the most part, to the results of standardized achievement and mental tests and school marks.

2. Information recorded should be as accurate and objective as possible.

3. A cumulative record system, to be truly effective, is regularly used by teachers in their daily work with pupils. This has several implications:

a. Records should be readily available to teachers. They are not fulfilling their proper function if teachers have to make a trip to the school office every time they want to use them.

b. Only information which will be used by teachers, counselors, or adminstrators should be included on the forms.

c. If teachers are to use the records, they should have a part in developing the items which are to be included. Two suggestions are worthwhile in this connection. Teachers should study their school objectives and the various means they use in evaluating these objectives. The forms should then be planned to include these items. Second, it may be worthwhile to study forms which are being used by other schools.[5]

4. Physical or mechanical characteristics:

a. The records should be as simple as possible to allow a whole picture of the pupil at a glance and to keep clerical work at a minimum. One good way to achieve this aim is to place as much information as possible in one long column across or down the card for each year's record, with the next year's record in the second column.

b. It may be wise to use the newly designed record in mimeographed form for a year or two until the staff has had time to perfect the form which will be most efficient for them. When it is finally printed, only a limited supply should be stocked so that further revisions may be made.

c. Only one folder or a series of cards integrated from level to level within the school system should be used so that records will

---

[5] Research Division of the National Education Association, 1201 Sixteenth St., N.W., Washington 6, D.C., will loan packets of sample cumulative records to teachers. The only charge is for return postage.

not have to be duplicated as pupils move from primary to intermediate, to junior high, and to high school levels.

d. Column headings should clearly describe information required.

e. There should be sufficient space for entries. Narrow spacing of lines makes it difficult to write entries legibly and, hence, makes reading of the record difficult.

f. All information should be placed on one card or in one folder with insert cards so that all data may be filed in one place. The only exception to such a practice may occur in larger school systems where several people have to maintain special aspects of information about each pupil.

g. Paper used for the card forms or folders should be durable, flexible, and, for minimum eyestrain, buff in color.

h. Flexibility should be planned for in the record system used. Extra space should be left for teacher notations. Space should be allowed for noting the location of information which is too bulky or too confidential to include on the regular card. Unlabeled columns or lines should be provided for entry of data which had not previously been anticipated when the forms were developed. Finally, the use of a folder allows for flexibility by permitting extra notations, rating scale sheets, samples of pupils' work, and so on, to be filed with the basic data.

i. Information should be summarized once or twice a year and as much bulky material as possible discarded. However, any detailed information of value, such as case studies, representative samples of work, and so on, should be kept.

Bibliography

Adams, Georgia, and Theodore L. Torgerson, *Measurement and Evaluation for the Secondary School Teacher*. New York: Holt, Rinehart & Winston, Inc., 1956.

Ahmann, J. Stanley, and Marvin D. Glock, *Evaluating Pupil Growth*. Boston: Allyn and Bacon, 1958.

Almy, Millie, *Ways of Studying Children*. New York: Bureau of Publications, Teachers College, Columbia University, 1959.

American Council on Education, *Helping Teachers Understand Children*. Washington, D.C.: the Council, 1945.

Association for Childhood Education International, *Learning about Role-playing for Children and Teachers*. Washington, D.C.: the Association, 1960.

Baron, Denis, and Harold W. Bernard, *Evaluation Techniques for Classroom Teachers*. New York: McGraw-Hill Book Co., Inc., 1958.

Bell, J. E., *Projective Techniques*. New York: Longmans, Green & Co., Inc., 1948.

Bonney, Merl E., *Mental Health in Education*. Boston: Allyn and Bacon, Inc., 1960.

Bureau of Educational Research, *A Guide to the Use of Anecdotal Records*. New York: Board of Education of the City of New York, 1955.

California State Department of Education, *Evaluating Pupil Progress*. Sacramento: Bulletin of the California State Department of Education, 1952. See also Revised Edition, 1960.

Cattell, Raymond B., *Personality and Motivation-Structure and Measurement*. New York: Harcourt, Brace & World, Inc., 1957.

Federal Security Agency, Office of Education, *Handbook of Cumulative Records*. Washington, D.C.: Government Printing Office, 1944.

Froehlich, Clifford P., and Kenneth B. Hoyt, *Guidance Testing*. Chicago: Science Research Associates, Inc., 1959.

Gronlund, Norman E., *Sociometry in the Classroom*. New York: Harper & Brothers, 1959.

Guilford, J. P., *Personality*. New York: McGraw-Hill Book Co., Inc., 1959.

Haas, Robert B., ed., *Psychodrama and Sociodrama in American Education*. New York: Beacon House, Inc., 1949.

Jennings, H. H., *Leadership and Isolation*. New York: Longmans, Green & Co., Inc., 1950.

Moreno, J. L., ed. *The Sociometry Reader*. Glencoe, Illinois: The Free Press, 1960.

Mouton, J. S., R. R. Blake, and B. Fruchter, "The Validity of Sociometric Responses," *Sociometry*, 18 (1955), pp. 181–206.

Mussen, Paul H., ed., *Handbook of Research Methods in Child Development*. New York: John Wiley & Sons, Inc., 1960.

Northway, M. L., *A Primer of Sociometry*. Toronto: University of Toronto Press, 1952.

Rohde, A. R., *The Sentence Completion Method*. New York: The Ronald Press Company, 1957.

Rothney, John W., Paul J. Danielson, and Robert A. Heimann, *Measurement and Guidance*, Chap. VIII. New York: Harper & Brothers, 1959.

Schwartz, Alfred, and Stuart C. Tiedeman, *Evaluating Student Progress in the Secondary School*. New York: Longmans, Green & Co. Inc., 1957.

Smith, Louis M., "The Concurrent Validity of Six Personality and Adjustment Tests for Children," *Psychological Monographs*, LXX, 4 (1958).

Strang, Ruth, *Counseling Technics in College and Secondary School*. New York: Harper & Brothers, 1937.

Torgerson, Theodore L., *Studying Children*. New York: The Dryden Press, 1947.

Torgerson, Theodore L., and Georgia Adams, *Measurement and Evaluation for the Elementary-School Teacher*. New York: Holt, Rinehart & Winston, Inc., 1954.

Ullman, C. A., "Identification of Maladjusted School Children," Federal Security Agency, Public Health Service, *Public Health Monograph*, No. 7 (1952).

White, Verna, *Studying the Individual Pupil*. New York: Harper & Brothers, 1958.

Withall, J., "The Development of a Technique for the Measurement of Social-Emotional Climate in Classrooms," *Journal of Experimental Education*, 17 (1949), pp. 347–61.

Wrightstone, J. Wayne, Joseph Justman, and Irving Robbins, *Evaluation in Modern Education*. New York: American Book Company, 1956.

Index